Somewhere Over The Gay Rainbow Lies The Truth

Telling Their Story in the "Gay"
Organization's Own Words

Is America Living a Lie?

For information address:

J2B Publishing LLC
4251 Columbia Park Road
Pomfret, MD 20657
www.J2BLLC.com

This book is set in Garamond.

ISBN: 978-1-948747-88-2

Somewhere Over The Gay Rainbow Lies The Truth

Telling Their Story in the "Gay" Organization's Own Words

Is America Living a Lie?

A collection of writings, letters, speeches, and publications of "gay" organization leaders and their critics.

Words and actions that have overturned America on the issues of homosexuality in our medical fields, our churches, our schools, and our laws.

This book is for education and information purposes only by the American Anglican Fellowship Inc., a non–profit organization.

Bradley Hutt

 J2B Publishing

Table of Contents

"Lest we forget at least an over the shoulder acknowledgement to the very first radical: from all our legends, mythology, and history, the first radical known to man who rebelled against the establishment and did it so effectively that he at least won his own kingdom--- Lucifer."

SAUL ALINSKY

"We can say again then that there is a commandment prior even to the Decalogue or the two Great Commandments, unspoken but implied in every page of scripture: "Thou shall be a truth-seeker" Only with that commandment in place do any of the other commandments make sense. If I am not a truth-seeker, if I do not have a teachable spirit, if I am not correctable by the evidence of fact and logic, then there is no hope of my ever coming to know either what is or Who is, let alone love Him with all my heart, mind, soul, and strength. Locked in my own self rightness, I will forever wander in darkness until death because I will not be open to hearing from He Who Is, the Source of Life."

F. EARLE FOX

Founder Emmaus Ministries

INTRODUCTION

The purpose of this book is to educate and inform inquiring minds how "gay" organizations changed America. We will use the gay organization's own words as they continue using their Saul Alinsky radical tactics to change the minds and rulings of the American Psychiatry Association, the Canons of the Episcopal Church, teaching in public schools, and in challenging laws in state and federal courts to normalize their lifestyle to citizens and families and gain acceptance in America.

The American Anglican Fellowship (AAF) has engaged in the debate on sexuality issues in the Episcopal Church since its introduction by the Integrity Organization in the seventies. The stated mission of the AAF and its members is to seek the truth in disputed matters and then provide information and education to all persons.

People of different views have debated homosexuality for decades. The issue has divided Americans and citizens around the world. "gay" organizations have gained public acceptance by forcing the issue in the courts and are now a designated group protected by federal law.

We also want to make a clear distinction between homosexual persons and homosexual organizations.

We believe that there are no "homosexual" persons as such, and that a homosexual orientation is a disorientation of personality, not an expression of it. So we will not normally refer to "homosexual persons" except to mean one who has a disorientation or engages in a behavior.

In fact, one cannot have a civil conversation with a friend or even a family member anymore having an opposite view. Most persons are so tired of the ongoing debate, that they have given up and accepted the issue no matter what side you take, because some consider it is a done deal; just like the gay organization's chant, "We're Queer, we're here, get over it."

I found out first-hand, an Episcopal Church Warden and delegate to diocesan conventions and as a member of the press to general conventions, where we were headed.

The Episcopal Church played an important role in the transition that overturned America, and its path and our nation's path are remarkably similar and parallel. Let's travel back in a time 49 years to 1972, when the Gay Rights Platform was introduced so we can better understand and educate ourselves regarding gay organizations, the purpose of this book.

THE 1972 GAY RIGHTS PLATFORM

Platform created at the National Coalition of Gay Organizations Convention held in Chicago in 1972

FEDERAL:

1. Amend all federal Civil Rights Acts, other legislation and government controls to prohibit discrimination in employment, housing, public accommodations and public services. (1972 Federal-1)

2. Issuance by the President of an executive order prohibiting the military from excluding for reasons of their sexual orientation, persons who of their own volition desire entrance into the Armed Services; and from issuing less-than-fully-honorable discharges for homosexuality; and the upgrading to fully honorable all such discharges previously issued, with retroactive benefits. (1972 Federal-2)

3. Issuance by the President of an executive order prohibiting discrimination in the federal civil service because of sexual orientation, in hiring and promoting; and prohibiting discriminations against homosexuals in security clearances. (1972 Federal-3)

4. Elimination of tax inequities victimizing single persons and same-sex couples. (1972 Federal-4)

5. Elimination of bars to the entry, immigration and naturalization of homosexual aliens. (1972 Federal-5)

6. Federal encouragement and support for sex education courses, prepared and taught by Gay women and men, presenting homosexuality as a valid, healthy preference and lifestyle as a viable alternative to heterosexuality. (1972 Federal-6)

7. Appropriate executive orders, regulations and legislation banning the compiling, maintenance and dissemination of information on an individual's sexual preferences, behavior, and social and political activities for dossiers and data banks. (1972 Federal-7)

8. Federal funding of aid programs of gay men's and women's organizations designed to alleviate the problems encountered by Gay women and men which are engendered by an oppressive sexist society. (1972 Federal-8)

9. Immediate release of all Gay women and men now incarcerated in detention centers, prisons and mental institutions because of sexual offense charges relating to victimless crimes or sexual orientation; and that adequate compensation be made for the physical and mental duress encountered; and that all existing records relating to the incarceration be immediately expunged. (1972 Federal-9)

STATE:

1. All federal legislation and programs enumerated in Demands 1, 6, 7, 8, and 9 above should be implemented at the State level where applicable. (1972 State-1)

2. Repeal of all state laws prohibiting private sexual acts involving consenting persons; equalization for homosexuals and heterosexuals for the enforcement of all laws. (1972 State-2)

3. Repeal all state laws prohibiting solicitation for private voluntary sexual liaisons; and laws prohibiting prostitution, both male and female. (1972 State-3)

4. Enactment of legislation prohibiting insurance companies and any

other state-regulated enterprises from discriminating because of sexual orientation, in insurance and in bonding or any other prerequisite to employment or control of one's personal demesne. (1972 State-4)

5. Enactment of legislation so that child custody, adoption, visitation rights, foster parenting, and the like shall not be denied because of sexual orientation or marital status. (1972 State-5)

6. Repeal of all state laws prohibiting transvestism and cross-dressing. (1972 State-6)

7. Repeal of all laws governing the age of sexual consent. (1972 State-7)

8. Repeal of all legislative provisions that restrict the sex or number of persons entering into a marriage unit; and the extension of legal benefits to all persons who cohabit regardless of sex or numbers. (1972 State-8)

1972 Gay Rights Platform, afaofpa.org/archives/1972-gay-rights-platform/Admin 2 May 22, 2010

http://www.rslevinson.com/gaylesissues/features/collect/onetime/bl_platform1972.htm

End

To the best of my knowledge, no one has told the story of the "gay" organizations' quest to normalize their sexual behavior and their critics responses to it by gathering and using their thoughts, words, plans, emotions, and actions.

Might it not be a good time to pause, pray, and listen to what these radical "gay" organizations are saying to citizens in their own words in telling their story that brought them front and center of everything in America?

Brad Hutt
Chair and Co-Founder
American Anglican Fellowship, Inc. 1984

1 – CONVERTING THE AMERICAN PSYCHIATRY ASSOCIATION

Inquiring minds might ask Robert R. Reilly, Author of, *Making Gay Okay*, what does psychiatry have to do with homosexuality?

His response is:

"Psychiatry purports to be and is recognized by law as a branch of medicine – that is, as a source of objective truth. Over the last forty years, it has been an instrument to justify and even to promote homosexual behavior. As will be seen the change from the diagnosis of a mental disorder to a symptom had nothing to do with science in the genuine sense. It has been the result, not of any discovery, but rather of pure political processes---indeed of power plays in meeting halls, restaurants, and bedrooms. The two sets of judgments stand on very different levels of science—one genuine and one not."[1]

Reilly states how these judgments changed because the:

"…authority of psychiatry is being used in lawsuits to establish the normality of homosexual behavior and to make the case for same sex marriage and adoption."[2]

His research reveals that in 1953, homosexuality was listed as a "sociopathic personality disturbance" in the DSM Manual by the American Psychiatric Association. In 1968, in DSM-II, the homosexuality listing had changed to "sexual deviation" which said in part:

"This category is for individuals who's sexual directed primarily towards objects other than people of the opposite sex, toward sexual acts…performed under bizarre circumstances…Even though many find their practices distasteful, they remain unable to substitute normal sexual behavior for them."[3]

"Gay" Activist Franklin Kameny, the man who President Barrack Obama singled out for special praise at a 2009 White House meeting, said: *"I feel the entire homophile movement… is going to stand or fall upon the question of whether or not homosexuality is a sickness, and upon our taking a firm stand on it."[4]*

The coalition of "gay" and woman's liberationists interrupted the national convention of the American Psychiatric Association in San Francisco to protest the reading of a paper by an Australian psychiatrist on the subject of "aversion therapy," a system of treatment which attempts to change gay orientation by keying unpleasant sensations (such as electric shocks) to homosexual stimuli. By the time, the meeting was over, the feminists were in charge...and the doctors were heckled from the audience.

[1][2][3][4] Reilly, Robert R. Making Gay Okay, First edition 2014 by Ignatius Press, San Francisco ISBN 978-2-62164-086-8

End

Psychiatrists, in a Shift, Declare Homosexuality No Mental Illness

By Richard D. Lyons Special to the NY Times

NY TIMES WASHINGTON, Dec. 15, 1973—The American Psychiatric Association, altering a position it has held for nearly a century, decided today that homosexuality is not a mental disorder.

The board of trustees of the 20,00D-member group approved a resolution that said in part, "by itself, homosexuality does not meet the criteria for being a psychiatric disorder." Persons who are troubled by their homosexuality, the trustees said, will be classified as having a "sexual orientation disturbance" should they come to a psychiatrist for help.

"We will no longer insist on a label of sickness for individuals who insist that they are well and demonstrate no generalized impairment in social effectiveness," the trustees said. "by itself, homosexuality does not meet the criteria for being a psychiatric disorder."

Persons who are troubled by their homosexuality, the trustees said, will be classified as having a "sexual orientation disturbance" should they come to a psychiatrist for help.

The semantics of the resolution and exactly how it differed from the association's previous position were challenged by reporters during a news conference at A.P.A headquarters. But association leaders insisted they had not given in to pressure from homosexual groups and that the difference in position was indeed real, rather than imaginary despite the apparent vagueness of their resolution.

Dr. Robert L. Spitzer, who is a psychiatrist at the Columbia College of Physicians and Surgeons, explained that "we're not saying that homosexuality is either normal or 'abnormal.'"

Many psychiatrists have held a traditional view of homosexuality as being a disease and regarded the best method of treatment as being an attempt to convert a homosexual to heterosexual behavior. If this occurred, the patient was considered "cured."

But the effect of today's action here would be to put psychiatrists on notice that some homosexuals—the exact number is not known—have adjusted to their sexual status and do not wish to change.

According to Dr. Spitzer, this would mean that many more homosexuals who need psychiatric help for reasons other than homosexuality would seek professional help because the homosexuals would know that the psychiatrists would not necessarily try to "cure" them by converting them to heterosexuality.

Deplore Discrimination

In a related action, the association's trustees adopted a resolution deploring discrimination against homosexuals in the fields of housing, employment and licensing.

Further, the board of trustees said it

"supports and urges the enactment of civil rights legislation at local, state, and Federal levels that would ensure homosexual citizens the same protections now guaranteed to others."

In addition, the board said,

"The A.P.A. supports and urges the repeal of all legislation making criminal offense of sexual acts performed by consenting adults in private."

Such laws exist in 42 states and the District of Columbia, according to the National Gay Task Force (NGTF), a New York-based homosexual activist group.

The NGTF hailed the association's action as "the greatest gay victory," adding, "The diagnosis of homosexuality as an illness has been the cornerstone of oppression for a tenth of our population." The fraction has been set far lower by other estimates.

Self-Appraisal

The NGTF said in a statement that linking homosexuality to mental illness "has forced many gay women and men to think of themselves as freaks."

"It has been used as a tool of discrimination in the private sector, and in the civil service, military, Immigration and Naturalization Service, health services, adoption and child custody courts," the statement added.

Dr. Alfred M. Freedman, president of the A.P.A., noted that the association's official list of mental disorders had classed homosexuality as a "sexual deviation" along with fetishism, voyeurism, pedophilia, exhibitionism, and others.

He said that whether homosexuality belonged there had been the subject of increasing debate, "fanned by the organized homosexual community, which has vigorously protested the prejudice that derives from classifying their condition as a mental illness."

Psychiatrists, in a Shift, Declare Homosexuality No Mental Illness, By Richard D. Lyons Special to the NY Times https://www.nytimes.com/1973/12/16/archives/psychiatrists-in-a-shift-declare-homosexuality-no-mental-illness.

End

Another article posted some 27 years later on the Human Life International (HLI) website in 2020 is extremely revealing of the relentless campaign used by LGBTQ organizations.

The article was written by Brian Clowes, PhD. He also concluded that the A.P.A. did not base their revised definition on scientific evidence, but that it was a purely political decision accomplished by militant activist gay organizations using guerilla like tactics to disrupt meetings and silence their speakers.

Another astounding fact pointed out in the article is due to the extreme political pressure exerted upon both the American Psychological Association and the American Psychiatric Association, no extensive public discussion on the mental pathology of homosexuality has been conducted since 1977.

The Homosexuals' American Psychological Association Coup

By Brian Clowes, PhD. August 4th, 2020

Homosexual activists often mention that the medical profession—specifically psychiatrists and psychologists—believe that homosexuality is a "normal human sexual response." In support of this assertion, they talk about how the American Psychological Association officially removed homosexuality from its list of "mental disorders" in 1973, and that the American Psychiatric Association also classifies homosexuality as normal.

What they do not mention, of course, is that these organizations did not base their changes of opinion on scholarly studies or new scientific evidence. Their acceptance of homosexuality was purely political, the result of a relentless campaign of deception, intimidation, outright violence and unethical collusion between elitist APA/APA committees and activist homosexual groups.

History of the APA on Homosexuality

In 1968, representatives of homosexual rights groups approached leading psychiatrists and psychologists and began to lay the groundwork for the reclassification of their lifestyle as a normal and healthy manifestation of human sexuality. These activists recognized that such a move was necessary if they were to win public acceptance. After all, society would not look very kindly upon civil rights lobbying done by groups whose members were recognized as "mentally disordered" by the medical profession.

In the three years during which the American Psychological Association's "Homosexuality Task Force" was deliberating, it collaborated with numerous homosexual activist groups, including the Gay Activist's Alliance, the Mattachine Society, and the Daughters of Bilitis, while systematically ignoring organizations with views that disagreed with the activists.

At about the same time, Abram Kardiner, former Professor of Psychiatry at Columbia University, revealed, "A powerful lobby of 'gay' organizations has brought pressure on the American Psychiatric Association to remove homosexuality from the category of aberrancy. This is only one facet of the tidal wave of egalitarianism and divisiveness that is sweeping the country."[1]

Alfred Kinsey's colleague Paul Gebhard revealed that anyone who believed that homosexuality was a disorder was systematically excluded from being a member of the APA/APA Homosexuality Task Forces or from even being able to present his views or evidence to them. In other words, the Task Forces only permitted those people who shared their viewpoint to voice an opinion, so their conclusions were preordained.

But the homosexuals did not focus on the APA/APA organizations alone; they intimidated psychiatrists and psychologists all over the nation. While the Homosexuality Task Forces were preparing their reports, anyone who dared present documentation that homosexuality was a psychological disorder anywhere in the country was shouted down and even physically attacked at public forums or at local and national meetings of mental health professionals.[1]

For example, at the 1971 American Psychiatric Association national convention, hordes of homosexuals screamed at "anti-gay" speakers. Activist Frank Kameny seized the microphone in the middle of one doctor's talk and shouted, "Psychiatry is the enemy incarnate. Psychiatry has waged a relentless war of extermination against us. You may take this as a declaration of war against you."[2]

Gangs of homosexuals roamed the exhibit hall and destroyed any literature they deemed not sufficiently "gay friendly." One psychiatrist wrote:

> *Using forged credentials, gay activists gained access to the exhibit area and coming across a display marketing aversive conditioning technique for the treatment of homosexuals, demanded its removal.* Threats were made against the exhibitor, who was told that unless his booth was dismantled, it would be torn down. After frantic behind-the-scenes consultations, and in an effort to avoid violence, the convention leadership agreed to have the booth removed. [2]

From this moment onward, the American Psychiatric Association was dominated by homosexual threats, violence and intimidation.

This systematic campaign of violence, propaganda and intimidation began to pay off in 1972. The National Institute of Mental Health's (NIMH) Homosexuality Task Force Final Report parroted Alfred Kinsey's discredited finding that "exclusive heterosexuality" and "exclusive homosexuality" were "sexual extremes," and that most people were basically bisexual. [3]

The NIMH report in turn exerted a great deal of influence on both APAs. In order to make its final report appear scientific, the American Psychiatric Association's Homosexuality Task Force sent a letter to all APA member psychiatrists. This letter did not ask whether or not homosexuality should or should not be declared "normal." It directed all members to vote that homosexuality was equivalent to normal sexuality. The letter did not, of course, reveal the fact that it was written and funded by the National Gay Task Force (NGTF). One of the letter's signers, in fact, later confessed that he knew that such knowledge would have been the "kiss of death" for a pro-homosexual vote. [2]

Despite the atrocious amount of manipulation behind the vote, the psychiatrists declared homosexuality normal by only a very slim margin. Subsequently, the APA eliminated homosexuality as a mental disorder from the 1973 edition of its Diagnostic and Statistical Manual (DSM).

APA member Dr. Henry W. Riecken wrote a scathing dissent in the appendix to the NIMH report entitled "Detailed Reservations Regarding the Task Force Recommendations on Social Policy":

> It is as if they [the Task Force] said, "Here is a phenomenon about which we know almost nothing and about which there is a great deal of anxiety and concern; therefore, let us suggest a major revision in public policy for dealing with this phenomenon." I cannot escape the belief that this is an utterly unreasonable conclusion to draw from the sea of ignorance and misinformation in which we find ourselves.

The essential point is that the change in the position of the APA on homosexuality was not brought about as a result of a careful regime of scholarly research and study; it was a blatantly political move, a pre-determined vote on the status of a mental illness. Furthermore, this vote was undertaken in a pervasive climate of deception and intimidation.

At no time before or since has any psychological or psychiatric professional group ever addressed any mental health question in this grossly unprofessional manner.

What Psychiatrists Really Thought

It is fascinating to see what psychiatrists really think about homosexuality when they are free from intimidation, threats of violence and political pressure. What was the true majority opinion of the APA on homosexuality?

Almost simultaneously with the 1972 NIMH report, the New York County District Branch of the APA's Homosexuality Task Force produced a second report. According to APA member Charles Socarides, M.D., the document concluded that homosexuality was a psychosexual disorder—but that it deserved civil rights anyway. [1]

It is even more revealing to examine the results of polls of psychiatrists taken since 1973 regarding the issue of homosexual orientation.

The original "voting" letter distributed by the APA Homosexuality Task Force in 1973 was answered by only about one-quarter of the recipients, obviously leading to a severe "volunteer bias" which led to pro-homosexual results. It is quite certain that, if all of the APA members had returned their "ballots," homosexuality would have remained a mental disorder in the view of the organization.

A later series of private surveys—which could be answered confidentially and without fear of retaliation—showed that two-thirds of APA member psychiatrists regarded homosexuality as abnormal despite the parent organization's switch. [1]

More specifically, in 1977, four years after the APA flip-flop, the journal Medical Aspects of Human Sexuality revealed that it had polled 2,500 psychiatrists on their view of what "current thinking on homosexuality" was, and, by a lopsided margin of 69% to 18% (nearly four to one, with 13% undecided), the respondents answered, "Homosexuality was usually a pathological adaptation as opposed to a normal variation." [4]

This is certainly a more accurate poll than the original APA letter, which was prey to all of the "volunteer bias" that self-selected populations exhibit. However, by comparison, the 1977 survey was truly random, and so its results should certainly be given more weight.

Due to the extreme political pressure exerted upon both the American Psychological Association and the American Psychiatric Association, no extensive public discussion on the mental pathology of homosexuality has been conducted since 1977.

Final Thoughts
Both the American Psychological Association and the American Psychiatric Association have become completely politicized organs of the left and endorse the entire range of rhetoric of the culture of death without exception. For example, both endorsed abortion even before the 1973 Supreme Court decision Roe v. Wade, and both have stated that post-abortion syndrome is non-existent.

The American Psychological Association has gone far beyond the legitimate practice of psychology and is now engaged in blatant political activism papered over with a gossamer veneer of medical terminology. According to one paper published in the APA's Psychological Bulletin, political conservatism is strongly associated with "dogmatism," "intolerance," "close-mindedness," "fear," "anger," "pessimism," "self-interest," "endorsement of inequality," "terror management," "lower self-esteem," "mental rigidity," "aggression," "disgust" and "contempt." [5]

Of course, there appears to be no attempt by the APA to chronicle the many possible psychological problems associated with liberalism. That would be an intolerable conflict of interest.

Endnotes:

[1] Charles Socarides, M.D. "The Sexual Deviations and the Diagnostic Manual." American Journal of Psychotherapy, July 1978.

Also see Arno Karlen. "Homosexuality: The Scene and Its Students." The Sociology of Sex. James Henson and Edward Sagarin, editors (New York City: Schocken Publishers), 1978.

[2] Ronald Bayer. Homosexuality and American Psychiatry: The Politics of Diagnosis (New York City: Basic Books), 1981, page 105.

[3] John M. Livergood, M.D. (Editor). National Institute of Mental Health Task Force on Homosexuality: Final Report and Background Papers (Washington, D.C.: United States Government Printing Office), 1972, page 2 (Introduction).

[4] Medical Aspects of Human Sexuality, November 1977.

[5] John T. Jost, Jack Glaser, Arie W. Kruglanski and Frank J. Sulloway. "Political Conservatism as Motivated Social Cognition." Psychological Bulletin (journal of the American Psychological Association), 2003, Vol. 129, No. 3, 339—375.

www.hli.org/resources/apa-on-homosexuality The Homosexuals' American Psychological Association Coup. By Brian Clowes, PhD | . 2020-08-04T15:43:54-04:00. August 4th, 2020. |

End

2 – SIEZING THE EPISCOPAL CHURCH WITH PAPER CANONS.

Armed with the new definition of homosexuality findings of the APA Psychiatrists, or rather the elimination of the term "homosexuality" itself and describing it as a perfectly normal way of life, the militant "gay" doctors and their followers turned to the church to seek out other like-minded LBGT church persons; and of course they selected the most progressive and richest church in North America, the Episcopal Church U.S.A. (TEC), the church of presidents.

This is an accounting of the biggest church takeover in world history. It is the story of a Newark, New Jersey based gay gang who devised a brilliant plot to influence the TEC by first gaining acceptance and respect then purposely infiltrating its key positions in a stealth operation of mind-boggling proportions.

The gang's goal was to acquire leadership positions and thereby gain control of a church comprised of nearly 7,000 Parishes and more than 3,000,000 members spread throughout the United States.

Liberal Episcopal churchmen, Diocesan Bishop John Spong, his assistant, Bishop Walter Righter, Dr. Louie Crew, and others from the Diocese of Newark, New Jersey were the principal enablers. Crew was a long-time professor at Rutgers University and the founder of Integrity Inc., a gay and lesbian organization in the Episcopal Church.

The Jersey Gang grew in numbers and organized TEC Gay Integrity Chapters in several states, and then infiltrated the ranks of the Episcopal Church at the local Parish and Diocesan Convention level, and the national level at General Conventions. The gang, when in possession of key leadership roles, were able to steer committees to modify or delete long held TEC positions and beliefs. They changed positions that formed the solid rock foundation of the Christian faith.

These changes created chaos and division, not only the Episcopal Church USA but in the world - wide Anglican Communion. Their highly controversial issues divided parishioners, divided families, and ending long-time friendships.

The Jersey Gang's Godfather was Louie Crew, aka "Queen Lutibelle" in gay circles. Crew was the founder of Integrity Inc., a national organization of gay and lesbian persons in the Episcopal Church. He was an Associate Professor at Rutgers University for many years.

Louie Crew was simply pure genius. He was a very kind, considerate and loving person who laughed at himself and others as he led the way for homosexuals, but he lived a lie by making a mockery of the truth.

His biography is extremely interesting, and it is printed in its entirety:

Biography of Dr. Louie Crew

"Dr. Louie Crew was born in the deep South in 1936. He received his B.A. degree from Baylor University, his M.A. degree in 1959 from Auburn and his Ph.D. from the University of Alabama in 1971. His dissertation was entitled "Dickens' Use of Language for Protest." In his career Crew has taught in England, Hong Kong, and China, as well as at colleges in Alabama, Georgia, South Carolina and Chicago in this country. He became Associate Professor of English at Rutgers University in 1989 and retired from that position in 2002. [1]

"Crew spent a momentous year of his early life in the U.K. He moved to London in 1965, at 28, having taught in U.S. prep school for six years, deeply in the closet. The Wolfenden Report had gone into effect for heterosexual prostitutes in the 1950s and had passed the first reading for homosexual persons just before he moved to England. The police knew the Report's section on homosexuals was likely to pass the second reading (as it did) and were not prosecuting. Crew welcomed the **chance to be far** enough from home not to embarrass his family if he were arrested and having lived in self-enforced celibacy to that point, he gave up on the idea of his attraction to men being a "passing phase." [1]

"Crew had been confirmed as an Episcopalian in 1961. In the U.K.

he immediately joined the Albany Trust (the polite name for members who did not want to write their cheques to "The Homosexual Law Reform Society") which was publicly supported by the Archbishop of Canterbury, Michael Ramsey. Crew interviewed for six jobs in the first week there and was offered jobs at all six. To that point he had taught privileged students in prep schools, so chose to go to the least privileged school of the six…He showed up on his BSA with tough work shoes he later learned the students were forbidden to wear. He notes that during his time in London he "went to 146 plays, 28 operas, and uncounted cinemas and symphonies...." [1]

"In 1974, Louie Crew founded the national organization for gay and lesbian Episcopalians known as Integrity. He served as editor of Integrity's newsletter from 1974 to 1977. He also co-founded the lesbigay caucus of the National Council of Teachers of English in 1975. He served on the board of directors of the National Gay Task Force (now National Gay and Lesbian Task Force) from 1976 to 1978. He also served on the Wisconsin Governor's Council on Lesbian and Gay Issues in 1983. [1]

"Crew's publishing activity is voluminous, from article to essays, from poetry to full length books. He wrote the first openly gay materials published in Change Magazine, Christianity & Crisis, Chronicle of Higher Education, The Churchman, Fellowship Magazine, The Living Church, Metanoia and Southern Exposure. He has been on the editorial board of the Journal of Homosexuality since 1978 (except for 1984 to 1988). He edited A Book of Revelations: Lesbian and Gay Episcopalians Tell Their Own Stories, a collection of 52 biographies, in 1991. His most recent publication is 101 Reasons to Be Episcopalian (Morehouse Publishers). [1]

"Dr. Crew has been a member of Grace Church in Newark, New Jersey, since 1989 and has served as a member of the vestry, a deputy to diocesan convention and as a member of the rector search committee. In the Diocese of Newark, Crew was a member of the Companion Diocese Committee with Hong Kong, a member and chair of the Task Force on Electronic Technology, a member and secretary of the Standing Committee, a member of the Cathedral

Chapter, a member of the Task Force on Minority Vendors, a member of the Resolutions Committee, a member and secretary of the Bishop Coadjutor Nominating Committee, a member of the Diocesan Council, the Diocesan Historiographer, a member of the Oasis Board, Co-Chair of the Oasis Search Committee, and a member of the Task Force on Episcopal Identity."[1]

[1]	https://en.wikipedia.org/wiki/Integrity_USA	Biography: Integrity USA

End

It appears Integrity forced acceptance of their elected lifestyle upon the church for self-serving means using the tactics of Saul Alinsky with not a shred of concern for the division, hurt, and harm it caused TEC laity. Why would an organization do such a thing? Where is their Love for their Brothers and Sisters in Christ?

3 – INTEGRITY - INFILTRATING THE EPISCOPAL CHURCH

Dr. Louie Crew was the founder of Integrity and the Godfather of the Jersey Gang in the gay takeover of TEC. Integrity members and their supporters, many of them who were active gay and lesbian Clergy, played the lead roles in the takeover by attending diocesan and national conventions as elected delegates, chairpersons, and members of key committees and boards. The Episcopal Church USA was under siege.

What Wikipedia fails to tell us is the manner of the takeover. It was well planned and rehearsed in great detail. Nothing was overlooked in the takeover of conventions and the adoption of new rules by resolution. This extended as far as the takeover (theft) of the vestry property and chattels of over 7,000 churches, worth billions of dollars that the national church paid not a penny for, because the property and chattels had been funded and built by the members congregations of each parish vestries.

Integrity USA [1A]

"Integrity USA is a nonprofit organization that claims to work with the Episcopal Church in the United States (TEC) for the full inclusion of LGBT members and their allies. Integrity was founded by Louie Crew in rural Georgia, U.S., in 1974. At its zenith, Integrity USA had been the leading grassroots voice for the full inclusion of LGBT persons in The Episcopal Church and for equal access to its rites, securing most of its goals in 2015.

Beginning in 2018, following a series of board resignations and controversy over allegations of recent mismanagement, financial misconduct, and lack of transparency, [1] the organization and its

19

future is a focus of scrutiny within the Christian press and members of the LGBT community. [2]

History

In 1974, Louie Crew who was on a teaching fellowship in San Francisco telephoned the reportedly progressive Grace Cathedral in that city, asking if they could help him and his partner meet other gay Episcopalians. The derisive laughter he heard in response prompted him to start a newsletter that November to help gay and lesbian members of the church support one another in what was then a fairly hostile environment.

A gifted writer, Dr. Crew penned the lead editorial himself:[3]

"Integrity derives from integer, Latin for 'entire.' All Christian wholeness demands affirmation of God ordained sexuality; and gays and straights alike are Charged with the responsibility of using their sexuality in healthy human sharing rather than perversely trying to change or exchange the Gift of God."

Across the country, people saw the newsletter advertised in both church and gay publications. They organized into a handful of chapters and gathered, 200 strong, the following year for a national convention. The newsletter grew into a magazine, which was published until 2007, by which time the Internet was providing more immediate, interactive and cost-effective means of communication with Integrity's members.

Often working in coalitions[4] with both secular and other faith-based groups, Integrity has been instrumental in advancing the claim LGBT persons are making for equal protection and opportunity. Through its many ministries Integrity stood at the forefront of LGBT acceptance[5] within The Episcopal Church and continued to work for progress towards full inclusion of its people.

Programs and activities, 1974-2018

General Convention

Integrity has had official representation at every triennial General Convention of the Episcopal Church since 1977. The organization's members have helped draft and gather support for the legislative resolutions by which the church's official stance has evolved from denial to tolerance to welcome.[6] The Integrity Eucharist at General Convention, once held on the margins, became an event that at its zenith in 2012 drew nearly 2,000 worshipers. Some resolutions towards equality that Integrity had helped to achieve included:

Official prohibition of discrimination against gays and lesbians in 1976.[7]

Ordination of the first openly gay priest in TEC in 1977.

Passage of a resolution apologizing for past "sins" against gay and lesbian people in 1977.

The General Convention spoke out against hate crimes based on sexual orientation and encouraged federal officials to take action against such violence in 1985.

Public denouncement of the then-popular belief that AIDS was "the punishment of God upon homosexual persons" in 1985.

A resolution explicitly affirming that gay, lesbian and bisexual people could not be refused ordination in the Episcopal Church for that reason alone in 1994.

The election, confirmation and consecration of the first openly gay bishop, The Rev. V. Gene Robinson in 2003.[8]

Passage of a resolution supporting the federal Employment Non-Discrimination Act (ENDA), inclusive of gender identity in 2008.

Adoption of four resolutions addressing gender identity and transgender individuals in 2009. Two of them supported enactment of civil sector anti-discrimination and hate crimes legislation protecting transgender people at local, state, and federal levels.

2018-2020: "Instability and Uncertainty"

Between March and June 2018, three Integrity USA board members resigned, leaving only one elected board member.

By Autumn 2019, Integrity USA was described by the Episcopal

News Service as "a shadow of its former self, beset by struggles with leadership, finances, and communication."[9]

In 2019, Integrity USA's board leadership had been described in the press as marked by "instability and uncertainty".[10] In late November 2019, Integrity USA's president resigned, citing the need to spend more time with her family.[11]

Integrity USA Founder Louie Crew Clay died two days later on November 27, 2019.[12]

As further appointments to the organization's board were made in contravention of the Integrity USA's bylaws, the legitimacy of Integrity USA's leadership and future elections have been placed in doubt by some remaining membership.[13]

In 2020, multiple former presidents called for Integrity USA's dissolution. [14]

References

[1] "Episcopal LGBT Advocacy Group Head Resigns amid Allegations of Mismanagement". www.christianpost.com. Retrieved December 8, 2019.

[2] "Facing financial struggles and board resignations, Integrity apologizes for lack of transparency". www.episcopalnewsservice.org. Retrieved October 18, 2019.

[3]"November 1974 [HTML]". Integrityusa.org. Retrieved March 11, 2017.

[4]Meredith Bischoff (June 12, 2012). "Organizational Partners of the Institute for Welcoming Resources". Welcomingresources.org. Retrieved March 11, 2017.

[5]"LGBT in the Church". Episcopal Church. Retrieved March 11, 2017.

[6]"Where The Episcopal Church Stands on LGBT Issues". Integrityusa.org. Retrieved March 11, 2017.

[7]"Acts of Convention: Resolution # 1976-A069".

Episcopalarchives.org. Retrieved March 11, 2017.

[8]"Acts of Convention: Resolution # 2003-C045". [9]Episcopalarchives.org. Retrieved March 11, 2017.

[9]"Facing financial struggles and board resignations, Integrity apologizes for lack of transparency". www.episcopalnewsservice.org. Retrieved October 18, 2019.

[10]"Facing financial struggles and board resignations, Integrity apologizes for lack of transparency". www.episcopalnewsservice.org. Retrieved October 18, 2019.

[11]"Episcopal LGBT Advocacy Group Head Resigns amid Allegations of Mismanagement". www.christianpost.com. Retrieved December 8, 2019.

[12]"RIP Louis Crew Clay, Integrity Founder and Champion of Inclusion, dies at 82". www.episcopalnewsservice.org. Retrieved December 8, 2019.

[13]"Integrity President Resigns amid Mounting Criticism". www.episcopalnewsservice.org. Retrieved November 26, 2019.

[14]"former presidents call for group's dissolution". www.episcopalnewsservice.org. Retrieved March 10, 2020.

[1A] https://en.wikipedia.org/wiki/Integrity_USA

Women's Ordinations

The LBGT Jersey Gang took a bold step in the highly controversial woman's ordination issue in the church by taking matters into their own hands and illegally ordained eleven women into the priesthood on July 29, 1974, in Philadelphia. Four other illegal ordinations followed later in 1975 in Washington, D.C.

These unauthorized ordinations created great controversy and divisions in the church and forced conciliation, in two distinctive directions without a shred of reconciliation, at the 1976 Episcopal General Convention. The Church was totally divided over the issues.

These renegade actions set a pattern for leftists to force an issue with uncanonical measures in a 'just do it' manner and we will take questions and face the consequences later. Shades of Saul Alinsky, and his do whatever it takes for change.

Twenty years later, in 1994 The Episcopal Church General Convention reaffirmed that both men and women may enter into the ordination process, but also recognized that there is value to the theological position of those who oppose women's ordination.

It was not until 1997 the Axe fell as predicted by the Orthodox Members of the Church. The General Convention reneged on its promises and declared that the ordinations licensing and deployment of women are mandatory.

Sea change number one, the deceptive deed was done. FORCED ACCEPTANCE DEMANDED! Zero consequences except for those who opposed the ordinations. Think about that for a minute.

Sex and the Jersey Gang

The Study of Human Sexuality, carefully orchestrated by the Jersey Gang members, was introduced at the 1976 TEC General Convention in Minneapolis. The resolutions read as follows:

Resolution Number: 1976-A068 Title: Re commend That the Church Study Aspects of Human Sexuality Legislative Action Taken: Concurred As Amended Final Text:

Resolved, That this General Convention recommends that the dioceses and the Church in general engage in serious study and dialogue in the area of human sexuality, (including homosexuality) as it pertains to various aspects of life, particularly living styles, employment, housing, and education.

Resolution Number: 1976-A069 Title: Recognize the Equal Claims of Homosexuals Legislative Action Taken: Concurred Final Text:

Resolved, That it is the sense of this General Convention that homosexual persons are children of God who have a full and equal claim with all other persons upon the love, acceptance, and pastoral concern and care of the Church.

Citation: General Convention, Journal of the General Convention of...The Episcopal Church, Minneapolis 1976 (New York: General Convention, 1977), p. C-109.

So the Episcopal Church, again pressured by the Jersey Gang, ventured into the unknown, calling for a study of homosexuality itself, as well as calling for equal rights of not 'all persons' but 'homosexual persons'. The Episcopal Church in its infinite wisdom at a general convention affirmed a Study of homosexuality and then declared that homosexuals are "Children of God" who deserve acceptance and pastoral care from the church. *It also called for homosexual persons to have equal protection under the law.*

A little known or remembered Amendment was offered during the debate/discussion to delete the term "homosexual persons are children of God" and replace it with "all persons are children of God". Let us think about that for a moment, was the adopted resolution just referring to homosexual persons exclusively or all persons to be children of God?

The amendment made perfect sense, why should the resolution not include all persons rather than just homosexual persons? It was the homosexual persons who sought inclusion in the church and the resolution excluded all other persons as children of God.

This became a huge point in later TEC discussions and conventions, "we are all children of God" proclaimed the church progressives, but in actuality they declared by resolution only homosexuals were Children of God.

Damn the torpedoes, full speed ahead said the Convention, it is all about homosexuality, it is not about all of us in the church, it is about the homosexual. And they pulled it off brilliantly.

The Jersey Gang Ordination pursuit included "The first openly homosexual priest, the Rev. Robert Williams, was ordained by the Diocese of Newark Bishop John Shelby Spong in 1989. The following year, Barry Stopfel was ordained a deacon by Bishop

Spong's assistant, Bishop Walter Righter. Because Stopfel was not celibate, but an active homosexual, this resulted in Canonical charges and a trial by Canon law.

The Church Court dismissed the charges some five years later stating that "no clear doctrine" prohibits ordaining a gay or lesbian person in a committed relationship.

"Despite these affirmations of gay rights, the General Convention affirmed in 1991 that "physical sexual expression" is only appropriate within the monogamous, lifelong "union of husband and wife".

In 1994, the General Convention determined that church membership would not be determined on "marital status, sex, or sexual orientation".

Conservatives raise their voices

The American Anglican Fellowship Inc. (AAF)., of Washington D.C., formerly Save Our Church Inc., is a group of Episcopalians in the Diocese of Washington D.C., formally organized in 1984 in anticipation of the Diocesan Convention's adoption of a resolution affirming "*The Koinonia Statement*" authored by Bishop John Spong of the Diocese of Newark, NJ. The Koinonia Statement declared homosexuality to be morally neutral and called for the blessing of same sex unions and ordination of non-celibate gays and lesbians.

Three members of Cursillio, (a church organization of laymen), James Brown, George Hooper and David Bickel, invited members of other Episcopal Parishes in the Diocese of Washington D.C., Mike Hathaway, Stuart Broad, Hal Goolsby Robert England, Bradley Hutt and others to meet with them. They began to hold monthly meetings at St. Alban's Church on the Washington Cathedral grounds. They called the group, "Save Our Church Inc." out of concern for the direction the leadership of the Diocese of Washington was taking regarding issues that threatened the unity of the church.

The Rev. Michael Hopkins, then President of the "gay" organization Integrity, and Vicar of St. Georges Parish, Glendale, MD presented the Koinonia Statement Resolution at the 1994 Diocesan Convention. His Integrity Organization members attended the convention as invited guests of Bishop Haines and they took seats among the delegates throughout the National Cathedral. The Delegates thought not much of it initially, until the voting commenced.

When called for presentation, Hopkins addressed the Convention from the Canterbury Pulpit *"because this was important to the gay community."* This was a totally unprecedented move and statement, for all speakers to this very day are required to address the convention from the floor microphone facing the President of the Convention with the elected delegates.

Despite the strong objections of many delegates, the convention defeated a substitute motion to allow the general membership of the diocese time to study the sexuality issues within their own parishes by a narrow margin of 111-93 and then affirmed the Koinonia Statement by a margin of 134-52. The gay guests were reportedly heard to have voted in every voice vote. The convention was a predetermined fixed outcome. When questioned during convention as to the effect of the adoption of the resolution, Bishop Haines and Chancellor Cooney stated that the affirmation was only "the mind of the 1994 Convention."

One priest, the President of the Standing Committee and the Rector of Christ Church, Accokeek, the Rev. Pegram Johnson, elected to press the sexuality issues upon his parishioners following the Diocesan Convention, admonishing dissenters from the pulpit as being "unloving, homophobic fundamentalists." This caused great dissention and division among the parishioners of Accokeek and lifelong friends started debating and quarreling with one another as they took sides on the issues and it split the Church.

A small group of orthodox members of Accokeek began to hold weekly meetings in the homes of parishioners in a desperate attempt to determine a solution to the issues that were causing schism in their parish family. They called the Save Our Church Officers to advise them on what was actually going on in the diocese and what they could possibly do to stop it from destroying their parish.

27

Ten Resolutions on Sexuality were submitted in response to the Affirmation of the Koinonia Statement at the following Diocesan Convention in 1995, 7 of the 10 resolutions were submitted by delegates who were members of SOC. A little-known fact is that the Diocesan Convention actually approved Resolution #2-on A Statement in Koinonia which states:

"RESOLVED that the 101st Convention recognizes Bishop Spong's Koinonia Statement as a document to study but does not affirm that statement as approved church doctrine" and further

RESOLVED that the Diocese of Washington recognizes the need for a there to be respect for the theological process of the General Convention and our church to determine matters of official church teaching and be it further

RESOLVED that the Diocese of Washington shall continue to follow church doctrine and teaching on sexuality"

After the convention, David Bickel and I were asked by Bishop Haines to serve on the Diocesan Committee to continue the dialogue. We were the only conservatives named to the 7-member group, and we were not allowed to discuss scripture in the dialogue because participants would take it "personal and possibly have their feelings hurt". Nevertheless, it was a good start for honest, open conversation, but it turned out to be the last session ever held.

Subsequent Diocesan Conventions proved to be more of the same. Bishop Ronald Haines allowed "dirty tricks" of parliamentary procedure to discourage debate on the issues. These issues were not limited to women's ordination or homosexuality but the basic tenants of our faith and unauthorized unilateral actions that threatened the unity of the diocese.

In 2009, the General Convention responded to societal, political and legal changes in the status of civil marriage for same-sex couples by giving bishops an option to provide "generous pastoral support" especially where civil authorities have legalized same-gender marriage, civil unions, or domestic partnerships. It also charged the Standing Commission on Liturgy and Music to develop theological and liturgical resources for same-sex blessings and report back to the General Convention in 2012.

The same General Convention also voted that "any ordained ministry" is open to gay men and lesbians. This vote ended a moratorium on ordaining gay bishops passed in 2006 and passed in spite of Archbishop Rowan Williams's personal call at the start of the convention that, "I hope and pray that there won't be decisions in the coming days that will push us further apart."

Opposition to the consecration of the first ever openly homosexual bishop, The Very Reverend Vickie Gene Robinson, led to the creation of the Anglican Church in North America (ACNA). It officially organized in 2009, forming yet another ecclesiastical structure apart from the Episcopal Church (TEC). ACNA represented more than 100,000 members in its 700 parishes. Episcopal Bishop Robert Duncan was elected as its Primate.

Five diocesan conventions voted to withdraw from the Episcopal Church: the Diocese of San Joaquin, the Diocese of Fort Worth, the Diocese of Quincy, the Diocese of Pittsburgh, and the Diocese of South Carolina.

Bishop Catherine Jefferts Schori falsely declared that Iker had "abandoned the communion" and joined with the local diocese in suing Iker and followers, seeking to reclaim church buildings and property. On November 16, 2009, the appellate court issued an order staying the litigation while certain procedural issues were decided by the appellate court.

Jefferts Schori had criticized these moves and stated that schism is not an "honored tradition within Anglicanism" and claims schism has "frequently been seen as a more egregious error than charges of heresy."

In Pittsburgh, one member of the Standing Committee remained in TEC and some members of each of the other governing bodies also remained. Those persons who chose to remain in TEC were falsely recognized as the Diocese by the Presiding Bishop and executive Council of the Episcopal Church.

A Virginia trial court had ruled in 2008 that the eleven congregations could keep their parish property when the members split from TEC. However, TEC claimed that the property belonged to it under their

Dennis Canon. After appeals reached the Virginia Supreme Court, a new trial was ordered that resulted in a decision returning their property to TEC due to a lazy bench of judges who did not want to get into a religious controversy. In fact, it went against the very same Canons of TEC to resort to any civil courts to settle a church dispute. Subsequent appeals by those who left TEC were unsuccessful including an appeal by one parish to the U.S. Supreme Court in 2014.

Other rulings in Colorado and California unjustly ordered congregations to return their properties to TEC. On January 5, 2009, the California Supreme Court ruled that St. James Anglican Church in Newport Beach could not keep property held in the name of an Episcopal parish. The court wrongly concluded that even though the vestry names were on the property deeds for many years and duly recorded among the land records of the state, the local churches had agreed to be part of the general church. A ridiculous ruling, for I served on the vestry for more than 50 years and the vestry members I served with barely knew their own parish by-laws, much less than their Diocesan and National Church Canons and by-laws

The Liberal Left in TEC had approved a paper Canon of Possession and Ownership of all church buildings, all 7,000 of them in 1979. Not a canon to fire cannonballs at enemies in wartime, but a Church Canon or Law. A Paper Canon the Leftists themselves created in a stealth operation on a Convention floor where few of the 1,500 delegates knew or cared about what was going on in the plethora of resolutions and amendments being considered on the floor and behind the scenes with little opposition. Funny thing though, any and all recordings and records of the actual speeches and voting were lost long ago.

The now infamous "Dennis Canon" sailed through the approval process out of Committee and onto the floor for a vote despite protests by conservatives who saw through the scheme and precise wording. The Canon was falsely presented to the delegates at The 1979 Episcopal Church General Convention as a means of bringing the Dioceses and their churches together under an Umbrella Policy to protect their properties with lower insurance rates, lower hospitalization and retirement costs. It was "Great News" for everyone! Church vestries would be saving money for their insurance, hospitalization and retirement programs.

Bishop John Walker told me personally it was very good news, and that we would be very happy with it and I believed him.

What fools we both were! We were bamboozled by leftists with lies and by a canon they created as the instrument to carry out their long-range plan and scheme.

It was common for insurance companies to provide discounted rates to large organizations and companies, but they had a very understandable requirement. In order for the organization to obtain the attractive discounted rates under an umbrella policy the organization (i.e. TEC) must own the property covered by the umbrella policy.

TEC at that time did not own any property. The owner of all church property was the Vestry, their elected governing body, and rightly so; for the Vestry not only organized the founding of their church, but they also either physically built the buildings, or mortgaged their homes to build their church buildings. Church property was recorded like all other property in the land records of the county and state by deed and trust.

TEC leadership then conspired to gain complete ownership and control of 7,000 church properties. They wrote a new Canon for approval by TEC General Convention and touted the Canon as a huge benefit for all parishes when in reality it confiscated all Vestry property. The Rt. Rev. Walter D. Dennis, former Suffragan Bishop of New York, a lawyer and civil rights activist proposed its adoption as a Canon at General Convention.

The "Dennis" Canon I.7.4 reads as follows:

"All real and personal property held by or for the benefit of any Parish, Mission or Congregation is held in trust for this Church and the Diocese thereof in which such Parish, Mission or Congregation is located. The existence of this trust, however, shall in no way limit the power and authority of the Parish, Mission or Congregation otherwise existing over such property so long as the particular Parish, Mission or Congregation remains a part of, and subject to, this Church

and its Constitution and Canons."

"….So long as the particular Parish, Mission or Congregation remains part of. And subject to, this Church and its Constitution and Canons."

This Canon, voted on by a single convention, thrust a dagger into the hearts of 7,000 TEC Vestries as it relieved them, without their knowledge or consent, of all their property, buildings, and chattels.

End

Believe it or not, the Vestry signatures on the church deed of the land records in their County Court Houses now meant nothing.

The stealth operation was a total victory for the liberal left, and it was accomplished without the approval of 7,000 church vestries who were never notified of this issue.

4 - REDEFINING MARRIAGE FOR AMERICA

Episcopal bishops told their members that they would never approve of same sex marriage. They said marriage was a sacrament of the church and only between a man and a woman. They said the only same-sex relationship they would recognize were same sex <u>unions</u> in a lifelong monogamist relationship. Then Episcopal bishops betrayed the laity of the Episcopal Church with Canon I.18, redefined marriage for the Episcopal Church and sealed the doors of the Supreme Court ruling of same sex marriage with all the rights and privileges thereto.

The following is a true copy of Canon I.18 of the Episcopal Church USA Constitution and Canons.

Canon I.18 of the Episcopal Church USA Constitution and Canons.

Resolved, the House of Deputies concurring, That Canon I.18 is hereby amended to read as follows:

CANON 18: Of the Solemnization of Holy Matrimony

Canon 18: Of the Celebration and Blessing of Marriage

Sec. 1. Every Member of the Clergy of this Church shall conform to the laws of the State governing the creation of the civil status of marriage, and also to the laws of this Church governing these canons concerning the solemnization of marriage Holy Matrimony. Members of the Clergy may solemnize a marriage using any of the liturgical forms authorized by this Church.

Sec. 2. Before solemnizing a marriage the Member of the Clergy shall have ascertained:

(a) That both parties have the right to contract a marriage according to the laws of the State.

(b) That both parties understand that Holy Matrimony is a physical and spiritual union of a man and a woman, entered into within the community of faith, by mutual consent of heart, mind, and will, and with intent that it be lifelong.

(c) That both parties freely and knowingly consent to such marriage, without fraud, coercion, mistake as to identity of a partner, or mental reservation.

(d) That at least one of the parties has received Holy Baptism.

(e) That both parties have been instructed as to the nature, meaning, and purpose of Holy Matrimony by the Member of the Clergy, or that they have both received such instruction from persons known by the Member of the Clergy to be competent and responsible.

Sec. 2. The couple shall notify the Member of the Clergy of their intent to marry at least no less than thirty days prior to the solemnization; Provided, that if one of the parties is a member of the Congregation of the Member of the Clergy, or both parties can furnish satisfactory evidence of the need for shortening the time, this requirement can be waived for weighty cause; in which case the Member of the Clergy shall immediately report this action in writing to the Bishop.

Sec. 3. No Member of the Clergy of this Church shall solemnize any marriage unless the following procedures are complied with:

(a) The intention of the parties to contract marriage shall have been signified to the Member of the Clergy at least thirty days before the service of solemnization; Provided, that for weighty cause, this requirement may be dispensed with if one of the parties is a member of the Congregation of the Member of the Clergy or can furnish satisfactory evidence of responsibility. In case the thirty days' notice is waived, the Member of the Clergy shall report such action in writing to the Bishop immediately.

(b) There shall be present at least two witnesses to the solemnization of marriage.

(c) The Member of the Clergy shall record in the proper register the date and place of the marriage, the names of the parties and their parents, the age of the parties, their residences, and their Church status; the witnesses and the Member of the Clergy shall sign the record.

(d) The Member of the Clergy shall have required that the parties sign the following declaration:

(e) "We, A.B. and C.D., desiring to receive the blessing of Holy Matrimony in the Church, do solemnly declare that we hold marriage to be a lifelong union of husband and wife as it is set forth in the Book of Common Prayer.

(f) "We believe that the union of husband and wife, in heart, body, and mind, is intended by God for their mutual joy; for the help and comfort given one another in prosperity and adversity; and, when it is God's will, for the procreation of children and their nurture in the knowledge and love of the Lord.

(g) "And we do engage ourselves, so far as in us lies, to make our utmost effort to establish this relationship and to seek God's help thereto."

Sec. 3. Prior to the solemnization, the Member of the Clergy shall determine, and shall require the couple to sign a declaration attesting

(a) that both parties have the right to marry according to the laws of the State and consent to do so freely, without fraud, coercion, mistake as to the identity of either, or mental reservation; and

(b) that at least one of the parties is baptized; and

(c) that both parties have been instructed by the Member of the Clergy, or a person known by the Member of the Clergy to be competent and responsible, in the rights, duties, and responsibilities of marriage as embodied in the marriage vows: that the covenant of marriage is unconditional, mutual, exclusive, faithful, and lifelong; and (d)that both parties understand these duties and responsibilities, and engage to make the utmost effort, with the help of God and the support of the community, to accept and perform them.

Sec. 3. Prior to the solemnization, the Member of the Clergy shall determine:

(a) that both parties have the right to marry according to the laws of the State and consent to do so freely, without fraud, coercion, mistake as to the identity of either, or mental reservation; and

(b) that at least one of the parties is baptized; and

(c) that both parties have been instructed by the Member of the Clergy, or a person known by the Member of the Clergy to be competent and responsible, in the nature, purpose, and meaning, as well as the rights, duties and responsibilities of marriage as embodied in the marriage vows: that the covenant of marriage is unconditional, mutual, exclusive, faithful, and lifelong; and

(d) that both parties understand these duties and responsibilities, and engage to make the utmost effort, with the help of God and the support of the community, to accept and perform them.

Sec. 4. Prior to the solemnization, the parties shall sign the following Declaration of Intention:

We understand the teaching of the church that God's purpose for our marriage is for our mutual joy, for the help and comfort we will give to each other in prosperity and adversity, and, when it is God's will, for the gift and heritage of children and their nurture in the knowledge and love of God. We also understand that our marriage is to be unconditional, mutual, exclusive, faithful, and lifelong; and we engage to make the utmost effort to accept these gifts and fulfill these duties, with the help of God and the support of our community.

Sec. 4. It shall be within the discretion of any Member of the Clergy of this Church to decline to solemnize any marriage.

Sec. 4. Sec. 5. At least two witnesses shall be present at the solemnization, and together with the Member of the Clergy and the parties, sign the record of the solemnization in the proper register;

which record shall include the date and place of the solemnization, the names of the witnesses, the parties and their parents, the age of the parties, Church status, and residence(s).

Sec. 5. Sec. 6. A Member of the Clergy bishop or priest may pronounce a blessing upon a civil marriage using any of the liturgical forms authorized by this Church.

Sec. 4 Sec. 7. It shall be within the discretion of any Member of the Clergy of this Church to decline to solemnize or bless any marriage and be it further.

Resolved that this canon shall become effective on the First Sunday of Advent, 2015."

End

Hundreds of years of the definition of Holy Matrimony altered by the vote of a single Episcopal Church convention. A convention that was bamboozled by a gay organization using self-serving presentations, bully pulpit tactics, and dirty political tricks to bring about the convention vote. The gay organizations forced the issue upon the members of TEC without Christian consensus.

Think about it for a moment. This was not a decision to be made by a single convention. Is TEC, their clergy and members living a lie? Has the TEC upheld the faith?

5 – THE LEADER OF THE CONSPIRACY

A Manifesto by John Shelby Spong

A Manifesto! The Time Has Come!

MelWhite.org

John Shelby Spong

"I have made a decision. I will no longer debate the issue of homosexuality in the church with anyone. I will no longer engage the biblical ignorance that emanates from so many right-wing Christians about how the Bible condemns homosexuality, as if that point of view still has any credibility. I will no longer discuss with them or listen to them tell me how homosexuality is "an abomination to God," about how homosexuality is a "chosen lifestyle," or about how through prayer and "spiritual counseling" homosexual persons can be "cured." Those arguments are no longer worthy of my time or energy. I will no longer dignify by listening to the thoughts of those who advocate "reparative therapy," as if homosexual persons are somehow broken and need to be repaired. I will no longer talk to those who believe that the unity of the church can or should be achieved by rejecting the presence of, or at least at the expense of, gay and lesbian people. I will no longer take the time to refute the unlearned and undocumentable claims of certain world religious leaders who call homosexuality "deviant." I will no longer listen to that pious sentimentality that certain Christian leaders continue to employ, which suggests some version of that strange and overtly

39

dishonest phrase that "we love the sinner but hate the sin." That statement is, I have concluded, nothing more than a self-serving lie designed to cover the fact that these people hate homosexual persons and fear homosexuality itself, but somehow know that hatred is incompatible with the Christ they claim to profess, so they adopt this face-saving and absolutely false statement. I will no longer temper my understanding of truth in order to pretend that I have even a tiny smidgen of respect for the appalling negativity that continues to emanate from religious circles where the church has for centuries conveniently perfumed its ongoing prejudices against blacks, Jews, women and homosexual persons with what it assumes is "high-sounding, pious rhetoric." The day for that mentality has quite simply come to an end for me. I will personally neither tolerate it nor listen to it any longer. The world has moved on, leaving these elements of the Christian Church that cannot adjust to new knowledge or a new consciousness lost in a sea of their own irrelevance. They no longer talk to anyone but themselves. I will no longer seek to slow down the witness to inclusiveness by pretending that there is some middle ground between prejudice and oppression. There isn't. Justice postponed is justice denied. That can be a resting place no longer for anyone. An old civil rights song proclaimed that the only choice awaiting those who cannot adjust to a new understanding was to "Roll on over or we'll roll on over you!" Time waits for no one.

I will particularly ignore those members of my own Episcopal Church who seek to break away from this body to form a "new church," claiming that this new and bigoted instrument alone now represents the Anglican Communion. Such a new ecclesiastical body is designed to allow these pathetic human beings, who are so deeply locked into a world that no longer exists, to form a community in which they can continue to hate gay people, distort gay people with their hopeless rhetoric and to be part of a religious fellowship in which they can continue to feel justified in their homophobic prejudices for the rest of their tortured lives. Church unity can never be a virtue that is preserved by allowing injustice, oppression and psychological tyranny to go unchallenged.

In my personal life, I will no longer listen to televised debates conducted by "fair-minded" channels that seek to give "both sides" of this issue "equal time." I am aware that these stations no longer give equal time to the advocates of treating women as if they are the property of men or to the advocates of reinstating either segregation or slavery, despite the fact that when these evil institutions were coming to an end the Bible was still being quoted frequently on each of these subjects. It is time for the media to announce that there are no longer two sides to the issue of full humanity for gay and lesbian people. There is no way that justice for homosexual people can be compromised any longer.

I will no longer act as if the Papal office is to be respected if the present occupant of that office is either not willing or not able to inform and educate himself on public issues on which he dares to speak with embarrassing ineptitude. I will no longer be respectful of the leadership of the Archbishop of Canterbury, who seems to believe that rude behavior, intolerance and even killing prejudice is somehow acceptable, so long as it comes from third-world religious leaders, who more than anything else reveal in themselves the price that colonial oppression has required of the minds and hearts of so many of our world's population. I see no way that ignorance and truth can be placed side by side, nor do I believe that evil is somehow less evil if the Bible is quoted to justify it. I will dismiss as unworthy of any more of my attention the wild, false and uninformed opinions of such would-be religious leaders as Pat Robertson, James Dobson, Jerry Falwell, Jimmy Swaggart, Albert Mohler, and Robert Duncan. My country and my church have both already spent too much time, energy and money trying to accommodate these backward points of view when they are no longer even tolerable.

I make these statements because it is time to move on. The battle is over. The victory has been won. There is no reasonable doubt as to what the final outcome of this struggle will be. Homosexual people will be accepted as equal, full human beings, who have a legitimate claim on every right that both church and society have to offer any of us. Homosexual marriages will become legal, recognized by the state and pronounced holy by the church. "Don't ask, don't tell" will be dismantled as the policy of our armed forces. We will and we must learn that equality of citizenship is not something that should ever be submitted to a referendum. Equality under and before the law is a

41

solemn promise conveyed to all our citizens in the Constitution itself. Can any of us imagine having a public referendum on whether slavery should continue, whether segregation should be dismantled, whether voting privileges should be offered to women? The time has come for politicians to stop hiding behind unjust laws that they themselves helped to enact, and to abandon that convenient shield of demanding a vote on the rights of full citizenship because they do not understand the difference between a constitutional democracy, which this nation has, and a "mobocracy," which this nation rejected when it adopted its constitution. We do not put the civil rights of a minority to the vote of a plebiscite.

I will also no longer act as if I need a majority vote of some ecclesiastical body in order to bless, ordain, recognize and celebrate the lives and gifts of gay and lesbian people in the life of the church. No one should ever again be forced to submit the privilege of citizenship in this nation or membership in the Christian Church to the will of a majority vote.

The battle in both our culture and our church to rid our souls of this dying prejudice is finished. A new consciousness has arisen. A decision has quite clearly been made. Inequality for gay and lesbian people is no longer a debatable issue in either church or state. Therefore, I will from this moment on refuse to dignify the continued public expression of ignorant prejudice by engaging it. I do not tolerate racism or sexism any longer. From this moment on, I will no longer tolerate our culture's various forms of homophobia. I do not care who it is who articulates these attitudes or who tries to make them sound holy with religious jargon.

I have been part of this debate for years, but things do get settled and this issue is now settled for me. I do not debate any longer with members of the "Flat Earth Society" either. I do not debate with people who think we should treat epilepsy by casting demons out of the epileptic person; I do not waste time engaging those medical opinions that suggest that bleeding the patient might release the infection. I do not converse with people who think that Hurricane Katrina hit New Orleans as punishment for the sin of being the birthplace of Ellen DeGeneres or that the terrorists hit the United

Sates on 9/11 because we tolerated homosexual people, abortions, feminism or the American Civil Liberties Union. I am tired of being embarrassed by so much of my church's participation in causes that are quite unworthy of the Christ I serve or the God whose mystery and wonder I appreciate more each day. Indeed I feel the Christian Church should not only apologize but do public penance for the way we have treated people of color, women, adherents of other religions and those we designated heretics, as well as gay and lesbian people.

Life moves on. As the poet James Russell Lowell once put it more than a century ago: "New occasions teach new duties, Time makes ancient good uncouth." I am ready now to claim the victory. I will from now on assume it and live into it. I am unwilling to argue about it or to discuss it as if there are two equally valid, competing positions any longer. The day for that mentality has simply gone forever.

This is my manifesto and my creed. I proclaim it today. I invite others to join me in this public declaration. I believe that such a public outpouring will help cleanse both the church and this nation of its own distorting past. It will restore integrity and honor to both church and state. It will signal that a new day has dawned, and we are ready not just to embrace it, but also to rejoice in it and to celebrate it.

– John Shelby Spong, Retired Episcopal Bishop

[1] https://melwhite.org/a-manifesto-by-john-shelby-spong/

End

My response to the Spong Manifesto is, "Why did you not break away from the Episcopal Church and form a new church Bishop Spong?" It would have been the right thing to do, and a means to break away from the church in an honorable and peaceful fashion, totally avoiding conflict and the hurt it caused to the silent members in the pews. And equally as important, a move that has been proven to build the church, not destroy it.

I found the following article by Dr. Albert Mohler to be very straight forward in his response to Spong's manifesto that the debate over homosexuality is over, and he will no longer debate members of the "Flat Earth Society," disparaging those who uphold the Tenets of the

Christian Faith.

The Battle is Over?—Bishop Spong Exits the Debate

Albert Mohler - October 20, 2009 - albertmohler.com

"The battle is over. The victory has been won. There is no reasonable doubt as to what the final outcome of the struggle will be." Those are the words of John Shelby Spong, the retired Episcopal bishop of Newark, New Jersey. In his recently released "manifesto," Bishop Spong declares, "it is time to move on," and pledges never again to debate the issues of homosexuality or homosexual rights.

John Shelby Spong's new manifesto is a sign of the times. For the past three decades, Bishop Spong has staked out a theological position that is so far outside the realm of Christian orthodoxy that it defies description. In a succession of notorious publications, Spong has denied virtually every conceivable doctrine and has embraced almost every imaginable heresy. His abandonment of biblical Christianity is both intentional and straightforward -- what this bishop demands is nothing less than the total reformulation of the Christian faith. In other words, Bishop Spong would replace Christianity with a new post-Christian religion while continuing to be recognized as a bishop of the Episcopal Church.

An ardent proponent of gay rights and the total normalization of homosexuality, Bishop Spong has long pressed for same-sex unions and the ordination of practicing homosexuals to every office in his church. In his new manifesto, he simply declares victory for his cause. Though skirmishes in many churches and denominations continue, the bishop is convinced that the final outcome of the struggle is clear: "Homosexual people will be accepted as equal, full human beings, who have a legitimate claim on every right that both church and society has to offer any of us. Homosexual marriages will become legal, recognized by the state and pronounced holy by the church."

In an act of individual self-assertion, Spong simply declares that he no longer needs "a majority vote of some ecclesiastical body" in order to bless or ordain gay and lesbian people throughout the life of the church. "The battle in both our culture and our church to rid our souls of this dying prejudice is finished," he asserts. "A new consciousness has arisen. A decision quite clearly has been made. Inequality for gay and lesbian people is no longer a debatable issue in either church or state."

In the most interesting section of his manifesto, Bishop Spong announces that he will no longer debate the issue of homosexuality with anyone. "I have been part of this debate for years, but things do get settled and this issue is now settled for me," Spong explains. "I do not debate any longer with members of the 'Flat Earth Society' either."

Indeed, Spong has been a participant in debates over homosexuality for the last quarter century. Now, he simply announces that he will no longer debate the issue because he is no longer even willing to admit that there are two sides to the debate. I suppose I should not have been surprised to find my name listed among those he will never again debate.

Though Bishop Spong appears to mean that he will not engage in debate concerning homosexuality on any conceivable grounds, he is particularly clear that he will not debate the question of whether homosexuality is a sin. Those who claim that homosexuality is sinful or deviant are, Spong insists, simply "unlearned." He writes: "I will no longer engage the biblical ignorance that emanates from so many right-wing Christians about how the Bible condemns homosexuality, as if that point of view still has any credibility."

Of course, Bishop Spong rejects any claim that the Bible is the Word of God. He knows full well that the Bible comprehensively condemns homosexuality in any form as sinful, so when he refers to "biblical ignorance" he is referring to those who would understand the Bible to be the binding authority for the church. Belief in the Bible as the revealed Word of God, he makes clear, is simply ignorant.

One section of his manifesto reeks of unintended irony. He simply declares that the global debate over homosexuality has been terminated. "The world has moved on, leaving these elements of the

Christian Church that cannot adjust to new knowledge or a new consciousness lost in a sea of their own irrelevance. They no longer talk to anyone but themselves."

The obvious irony is this -- the churches and denominations that have most eagerly embraced the normalization of homosexuality are also those losing members by the millions. While the Episcopal Church in the United States is following the dictates of Bishop Spong and his apostate colleagues, that denomination has lost entire dioceses, along with a huge swath of its membership. Meanwhile, the conservative and orthodox churches in the Anglican Communion are thriving, growing, and emboldened. So, which churches are "lost in a sea of their own irrelevance?"

Bishop Spong clearly hopes that his new manifesto will bring all debate over homosexuality to an end. Not hardly. While the bishop's manifesto is written in the language of bravado, it actually represents an intellectual posture of surrender. Worldwide, the percentage of churches and denominations that have embraced Bishop Spong's position on homosexuality is infinitesimally small. The Episcopal Church has taken radical steps to abandon biblical sexuality, but even within that denomination the debate over sexuality is hardly over.

If, as we should expect, Bishop Spong is true to his word, he will be missing from any future debate over the question of homosexuality. That debate will continue without him. Nevertheless, we should note carefully his effort to marginalize and silence those committed to a biblical understanding of homosexuality. While Bishop Spong's manifesto is nothing to fear, the effort to silence all opposition to the normalization of homosexuality will undoubtedly continue.

And so, Bishop Spong exits the debate. And yet, given what we have come to expect of John Shelby Spong, I'm betting we haven't heard the last from him yet.

R. Albert Mohler, Jr.

[1]https://albertmohler.com/2009/10/20/the-battle-is-over-bishop-spong-exits-the-debate

End - Amen good pastor.

6 – ATTACKING MAINSTREAM CHRISTIAN MINISTRIES

This is another showing the strategy of gay organizations is to relentlessly attack mainstream Christian ministries to force acceptance of same sex relationships even in teen and young adult groups. Throughout history, church members who disagree with church leadership or doctrine usually split off from the mainline denomination and form a new church. Homosexuals have refused to leave and form their own denomination electing instead to stay and demand the denomination change and accept their chosen lifestyle. They have done this in spite of the division, hurt, suffering, and pain it causes to friends in Christ? Why?

Critics Demand Young Life "Fully Affirm Queer Relationships"

juicyecumenism.com

By Jeffrey Walton

August 14, 2020 [1]

A prominent ecumenical Christian ministry is facing criticism from a group of former staff and volunteers who argue that the nearly 80-year-old organization should open leadership roles to those in same-sex relationships.

Young Life, the Colorado Springs-based parachurch ministry, operates camps and outreach to teens and young adults across more than 100 countries. It is unclear how extensive or organized the LGBT-affirming pressure campaign is. Religion News Service (RNS) reports [1] this week that it took shape in July as a grassroots campaign that has become a "movement" – citing more than 6,700 signatures for a change.org petition seeking for Young Life to repeal its sexual conduct policy.

It is unclear how many of the signatories have a connection with Young Life, which counts [2] approximately 348,000 youth "involved weekly around the world." The organization has a broad reach to students in middle school, high school and college. Further, special ministries seek to reach teen moms and teens with disabilities. Young Life counts "more than 80,000 staff and volunteers in 104 countries" and notes they minister to more than two million at any given time.

The petition makes several demands regarding claims to intersectional justice, but those regarding sexual identity and expression are the primary focal point. Petition organizers specifically state that Young Life must "Normalize asking for and using correct pronouns" and "Fully affirm queer relationships and queer sexuality."

"For many former Young Life employees, their break with the organization led to a break with their faith," RNS reports. Young Life describes its mission as introducing adolescents to Jesus Christ and helping them grow in their faith.

It is a legitimate question to ask why former staff or volunteers who now disavow the Gospel at the center of Young Life's mission want to continue in an organization whose primary purpose they have no interest in.

Young Life is not the first Christian ministry or parachurch organization to come under pressure from an organized campaign that seeks to open leadership roles to persons in same-sex relationships. In recent years, InterVarsity [3] and Cru have both been critiqued by former staff and volunteers who separated from the ministries after publicly identifying as gay or lesbian and pursuing noncelibate relationships, or affirming such unions.

In the past, small LGBT interest groups or networks have had a public relations roll-out (in this case, using the hashtag #DoBetterYoungLife) and received coverage from RNS. Some have fizzled without further coverage, others have gained broader attention.

Officials in a handful of other Christian institutions, including relief and development organization World Vision USA [4] and Azusa Pacific University [5], have made initial moves towards opening employment to those in same-sex partnerships, only to step back [6] after stakeholders and donors disagreed.

Hopefully, this campaign will not lead to an Azusa or World Vision scenario in which leadership changes policies, then flips back because of stakeholder outrage.

The RNS article leads with the story of Kent Thomas, a former mountain guide at a Young Life camp in British Columbia. Thomas, a man in a gay relationship, was told by Young Life that he could not continue in his role. Thomas tells RNS that almost six years later, that haunts him.

"I still have dreams about Young Life at least once a week," said Thomas, now 30. "Sometimes I'm being welcomed as a queer person, sometimes I'm being ostracized as a queer person."

As my colleague Chelsen Vicari observed with surprise, Thomas is not facing dreams about global pandemics, economic crisis, or bear attacks. Instead, weekly nightmares are about rejection from a student ministry years ago.

Officials within Young Life have sought to respond with a conciliatory tone, while maintaining orthodox Christian teaching.

"We are deeply saddened to know that any individual would walk away from their experience with Young Life feeling hurt or shamed and wish to apologize for instances where our sins of commission and omission have caused this pain," read a Young Life statement provided to IRD. "These stories highlight the need to review how we train staff and volunteers to come alongside and love kids who identify as LGBTQ+ — without conditions, judgement or shame."

In the statement, the parachurch group notes "Young Life welcomes and includes all young people as participants in our programs and activities, regardless of race, religion, ability, sexual orientation or identity, or other factors."

Young Life has added that "stories now being shared by current and former members of the Young Life family represent a small fraction of the experiences across Young Life" but does not dismiss the claims. The statement shares that on July 17, Young Life announced the creation of a council "to review all of these stories and recommend the appropriate course of action in each case."

The review council is to include both staff and non-staff.

"The formation of this council is a next step in what we expect will be a long process of review, reflection, repentance and reform," the statement reads.

The organization also notes that it "has expectations for leadership that are consistent with the tenets of our faith and what we believe is God's best for us. This includes an understanding that, at our foundation, we are all made in the image of a God who loves us. Young Life aligns with historical Christian theology in believing that sexuality is a gift from God and that God guides us in how to use this gift, including that intimate sexual activity should occur within a marriage covenant between a man and a woman."

Comments:

Comment by Lee on August 14, 2020 at 9:09 am
"It is a legitimate question to ask why former staff or volunteers who now disavow the Gospel at the center of Young Life's mission want to continue in an organization whose primary purpose they have no interest in."

And here is one answer to that question:

"Persons/Groups with gender-based, identity-driven agendas share a common DNA. When feeling disenfranchised, they move aggressively to insert their agenda into one that is not compatible. When, if not feeling fully welcomed in a way that requires the host to amend its' agenda, they act to force their way in. They can be relentless in that pursuit.

"Ultimately, if unable to amend the host entity to align with their beliefs, deconstruction of the host becomes their default agenda." (See e.g., the Boy Scouts of America, the United Methodist Church). As amoebas split, so do organizations.

"Hopefully, this campaign will not lead to an Azusa or World Vision scenario in which leadership changes policies, then flips back because of stakeholder outrage."

"It's more likely that the original stakeholders will merely shrug, abandon the organization, and reconstitute their mission elsewhere anew. (Southern Baptist Church congregations, for example, have done this often.)"

"As long as people are free to choose that which they will support, some will do so.

And, Young Life becomes Young LGBTQ Life, and life goes on."

Comment by Jeffrey on August 14, 2020 at 11:01 am
"Hello Lee, it does not appear that Young Life is going to cave. Glancing at the change.org petition, I'm not seeing a significant number of signatures added since publication of the RNS article. Young Life officials have the benefit of World Relief USA and Azusa's negative examples to learn from. I disagree with the RNS characterization of this as a "movement" (hence my skeptical quote marks) — a true movement would launch an organization(s) of its own, and I'm not seeing a serious call for an LGBTQ-affirming alternative to Young Life."

Comment by Mark on August 14, 2020 at 9:48 pm
"I think Lee provides valuable insight. I think the goal of modern liberalism/progressivism is constantly shifting. There will always be dissatisfaction that sexuality has not gone libertine enough. There is a level of narcissistic self-gratification that most rational Christians cannot relate to. The ultimate consequence is self-immolation or self-destruction as described in Huxley's "Brave New World" or Crichton's "Terminal Man."

Comment by Lee Cary on August 14, 2020 at 11:47 am
"Jeffery, you may well be accurate re. the future of YL. But Progressives take the long view. Conservatives are limited to reacting. Post-birth abortion, euthanasia, multiple-partner marriages, youth-adult marriages — movements in those directions and others are well underway today. I don't think there is necessarily a limit to the agenda of the Liberal Progressive movement. I've seen it advance on several fronts in my 70+ years. They never give up. Conservatives tend to tire from resisting."

Comment by Mike on August 14, 2020 at 2:43 pm

"Unfortunately, any organization has a tendency to go liberal, especially one that has been around as long as this one. It takes continual revival to keep a ministry on track and faithful to its original calling and beliefs. And while Jesus has promised to build His church and protect and provide for her, He did not say the same thing about schools, hospitals, and parachurch organizations."

Comment by Gary on August 14, 2020 at 2:59 pm

"Advocacy" should not replace traditional Christian witness. Many youths are looking for firm foundations, not merely what's trending. Traditional organizations are often sought out as sanctuaries from today's ubiquitous sexualized agendas. There need to be safe havens, trustworthy folds, not every organization transformed into an incubus of moral confusion and concupiscence to satisfy advocacy.

Comment by Steven on August 14, 2020 at 3:23 pm

Speaking of the long view, in another generation or two most Protestant denominations will have been queered. I'm Catholic now. The Magisterium is the firewall Young Life doesn't have.

Comment by Mike on August 14, 2020 at 3:36 pm

"As a 25-year volunteer with YL, I certainly hope they hold firm to the Gospel of Jesus. Politics has no business infecting ministry.

Comment by Cody on August 14, 2020 at 3:39 pm

"I hope Young Life does not change its standards. I was not aware of Young Life until in my 20s but found it to be a creative organization like Youth Specialties. All groups needed to be rooted in the Scriptures. I think of Richard Niebuhr's book Christ and Culture. It takes courage to stand against the flow of culture. May God in his mercy send revival."

Comment by Mark on August 14, 2020

"I think Lee provides valuable insight. I think the goal of modern liberalism/progressivism is constantly shifting. There will always be dissatisfaction that sexuality has not gone libertine enough. There is a level of narcissistic self-gratification that most rational Christians cannot relate to. The ultimate consequence is self-immolation or self-destruction as described in Huxley's "Brave New World" or Crichton's "Terminal Man."

Comment by Diane on August 15, 2020

"Members and former members of YL describe it as a "second family," and a lifestyle. Many young people who join its non-discriminatory ranks seek to remain as volunteer leaders and paid staff. The website for the YL group in my community makes absolutely no mention of their discriminatory, anti-lgbtq policies. That's dishonest. They prey on unsuspecting children and then turn on them once they're hooked on being part of the YL family. The betrayal experienced when gay participants learn – only when they seek to be volunteer leaders or staff – that they aren't welcomed to remain in the family is nothing short of spiritual abuse. There are lgbtq former Young Life folks who are in counseling/therapy to deal with the pain of being ousted from the faith family that groomed them years earlier in their school years. I use the word "groom" because this is no different from adults who intentionally mess with kids' bodies – whether it's sexual, emotional or spiritual. Young Life knows exactly what it's doing. Their deception in luring unsuspecting kids into what becomes a nightmare is immoral. It's called manipulation of the vulnerable – kids, by definition, are vulnerable and are easily preyed upon by manipulative adults. The organization is reprehensibly calloused. The grooming and recruitment of vulnerable lgbtq kids is sadistic. It needs to stop. Every Young Life website needs to boldly and explicitly state that it discriminates against lgbtq people. They need to be held accountable. They are ruthlessly deceptive."

Comment by Douglas on August 15, 2020

Yes, Diane God discriminates against sinful behavior. Is victimism your way of life?"

Comment by Diane on August 16, 2020

"Even traditional United Methodists have enough sense to not engage in proselytizing methods adopted by Young Life. Young Life is a parachurch organization. It does not exist to support any denomination (though they'd like you to think otherwise). Unlike Jehovah's Witnesses and Mormons who take their proselytizing door-to-door, Young Life volunteers and staff intentionally lurk where kids are to be found. They volunteer in your kid's school, show up at sports events. They seek out the most popular kids and lure them to Young Life "Club" meetings. In turn, they encourage those kids to bring their friends. No parent permission is sought. Young Life volunteers enter your kids' lives without parental knowledge or permission. No reputable United Methodist or any other denomination preys on kids like this. Young Life's marketing makes a point of leaving out any mention of Jesus, Christ, or God in its name. It's websites

explicitly promise each and every kid — no matter who they are — a place where they can be themselves, a place to belong. That's candy, along with game-filled club nights, to teens desperately wanting to belong, to be included. My sister got hooked on the Moonies back in the 1970s in much the same way. Young Life has absolutely no mention of discriminatory policies on their websites. Additionally, Young Life depends on financial backing from businesses and communities, telling folks that they're trying to reach high risk kids. The kids in my community that belong to Young Life come from affluent, White families. There's a Young Life group at the local, 99% White, prestigious private school.

The issue is not unlike consumer fraud. Young Life is basically a bait-and-switch operation that uses deceit to swindle $$$ that could be going into church youth programs in the community. One community awarded Young Life a $15K grant. My community just gave Young Life a $5K grant. On Young Life's website in my town is the listing of a jewelry business as a Young Life supporter. The same business just posted a congratulatory message on their Facebook page to a same sex couple that bought matching engagement and wedding rings. The business owners are Presbyterians and are totally unaware that they're supporting an anti-gay organization.

Christians with integrity don't prey on kids in a dishonest fashion. Adults expect their money back and demand an accounting when they're scammed with false promises of a product. Young Life is no different. Their marketing needs to be held accountable. It's important to note that those protesting Young Life's recruitment tactics are both gay and straight. They realize too late they've been deceived with the false promise of inclusion. Because many Christians reject the use of scripture to damn whole classes of people, whether it be based on religious belief, sexuality, race or gender, the Young Life straight folks protesting are just as betrayed to learn Young Life does in fact discriminate (remember, Young Life markets itself to kids as non-discriminatory). The organization is, in fact, exclusive. I'm surprised that traditional United Methodists on this site are supporting Young Life. The United Methodist church has been clear on its doctrines and the division that's resulted. The only deception practiced by United Methodists was the ad campaign of "open hearts, open doors, open minds". Like Young Life's message of inclusiveness " no matter who you are", the Open Doors campaign in the United Methodist church lacked the same integrity. It was dishonest. I think traditional United Methodists might agree with me on this. It's no different with Young Life. Those protesting want Young Life to change and be inclusive, as it says it is — but if anyone has followed their conversations on social media for the last year, they simply want Young Life to be honest. Of course, if Young Life chooses honesty, it knows it'll lose financial support. The majority of Americans don't believe lgbtq people should be discriminated against. It's all about money when it boils down to it. The root of all evil."

Comment by William on August 16, 2020
No matter how many volumes are written on this, it all always circles back to the same basic question. Where is it written in Scripture that sexual relations outside those of a man and woman in marriage is permissible and not sinful?

Comment by Gary Bebop on August 16, 2020
A malicious caricature of Young Life has been posted in the comments. I trust that we recognize the hideous nature of the smear.

Comment by Thomas Brown on August 16, 2020 at 3:22 pm
Diane really needs a Snickers.

Comment by Diane on August 16, 2020 at 4:03 pm
I am reminded that circuit rider preachers held Scripture in high esteem, so much so that sermons preached to enslaved people on southern plantations were meant to demonize those that dared to disobey their master. God's wrath would be visited upon them on judgement day should they disobey this very clear reading of scripture, they were told. Disobeying one's master was big time sin that would send Black folks to an eternity in hell. That's what was preached by sincere, Christian people of the book. They were wrong.

Christians have long used "the very clear reading of scripture" to exert power and control over everyone but straight, white, Christian males. You are simply playing a worn-out song. It's recognizable. You have no reason to change your tune because to do so means you lose power over others. Like the circuit rider preachers on the plantations, power is a thrill. You think you're serving God just as surely as those circuit rider preachers did. God was on their side because scripture was absolutely clear and infallible. And scripture hasn't changed. Its interpretation has. Your interpretation is increasingly obsolete…you are losing power to exercise control. You thrash about, beating down those who disagree. You claim it's the devil misleading anyone who no longer believes as you do. But the devil could be in you, as much so as the devil was in those circuit rider preachers.

Comment by Tom on August 16, 2020 at 6:34 pm

As has been noted, the Bible is awfully clear about sexual relationships outside of marriage between one man and one woman.

"Christian" organizations that have ignored this have not experienced good outcomes. Think the PCUSA, the ECUSA, the ELCA, et al.

Comment by Rebecca on August 17, 2020 at 1:59 pm

This is to Diane; can you give a source for your circuit rider comment regarding preaching to slaves on southern plantations? I would like to see where I could look it up. Thanks.

Comment by Rebecca on August 17, 2020 at 9:00 pm

I sort of answered my own question. Although I haven't found any references to circuit riders preaching to slaves that they need to accept slavery, every state in the South has something on the history of the Methodist Church in southern states. So, a search such as "Methodists in Mississippi," or "Methodists in Texas," should bring a more balanced view of Methodism than that expressed above in the comment section. I've even seen examples of revisionist history on Methodism by Methodists on the web, so actual state history would be a better choice to learn something on the subject. The Methodists as a whole have nothing to be ashamed of as far as their distant past in America. Following the Bible as written is the only way to do things.

Comment by William on August 19, 2020 at 7:12 am

Have been waiting for 50+ years for a single "liberal Christian" to answer this very simple question:

Where is it written in Scripture that sexual relations outside those of a man and woman in marriage is permissible and not sinful?

Instead, they ALWAYS dodge the question by either changing the subject or use all sorts of tactics in order to discredit the actual clear and unequivocal Scripture as written.

Comment by Diane on August 20, 2020 at 12:31 am

The biblical understanding of marriage is not simply "one man and one woman". Anyone who reads the Bible knows that Christian marriage is established through an exchange of property between men. A father (male) gives his daughter to another male (daughter's intended husband) in marriage. In biblical marriage, a woman is subject to and the property of her husband. The sexual relationship in

Christian marriage is that of a male partner-owner who not only seeks a helpmate, but who implants a seed in his female-property's flowerpot or womb. The flowerpot's soil might be fertile or barren. Shame on the woman who is barren. That, too, is a biblical understanding of a woman's role in marriage. Notably, men are not referred to as barren in the Bible unless they're eunuchs.

Given this biblical understanding of male-female sexual relationships within a marriage, the Bible of course does not affirm same sex marital relations. One wouldn't expect biblical writers with such antiquated ideas to affirm same-sex marriage. Most Americans, including most Christians, don't regard women as property of their husbands or husbands as owners of their wives. The biblical understanding of marriage with gender roles defined as male owner-woman-property are now considered antiquated and abusive to women. Once this property/owner form of biblical marriage was abandoned, it's not hard to understand why the biblical mandate for opposite sex marriage has now been abandoned.

Comment by Steve on August 20, 2020 at 8:12 am

The primary purpose of traditional heterosexual marriage was and is to provide for the perpetuation of the species, and to protect and provide for spouses and children. Demographics is destiny; if a society doesn't reproduce, it goes extinct. I understand marriage has had patriarchal aspects in the past, but those aspects have been systematically removed over time. The primary purpose remains valid, important and necessary. Two parent families are well known to have better outcomes than single. All things being equal, boys do better if they have a male role model and girls if they have a female role model. Life might be simpler and easier if we only took care of #1 but that's selfish, anti-social and destructive. Part of growing up in a functional family is learning how to care about and for others. There is inherent dignity and worth in committing to care for your spouse and progeny as long as you shall live. Those who don't understand this may not have experienced this in their own lives. Even so, we do hear of people who, despite never had this in their lives, commit to provide it for their own children, a hopeful development. It's essential that other responsible caring parents serve as role models: if not during one's childhood, as an adult, as part of an extended community. Because raising children well isn't simple, easy or self-evident.

Comment by William on August 20, 2020 at 11:56 am

Ephesians 5:21-33 - Instructions for Christian Households

21 Submit to one another out of reverence for Christ.

22 Wives, submit yourselves to your own husbands as you do to the Lord. 23 For the husband is the head of the wife as Christ is the head of the church, his body, of which he is the Savior. 24 Now as the church submits to Christ, so also wives should submit to their husbands in everything.

25 Husbands, love your wives, just as Christ loved the church and gave himself up for her 26 to make her holy, cleansing[a] her by the washing with water through the word, 27 and to present her to himself as a radiant church, without stain or wrinkle or any other blemish, but holy and blameless. 28 In this same way, husbands ought to love their wives as their own bodies. He who loves his wife loves himself. 29 After all, no one ever hated their own body, but they feed and care for their body, just as Christ does the church— 30 for we are members of his body. 31 "For this reason a man will leave his father and mother and be united to his wife, and the two will become one flesh."[b] 32 This is a profound mystery—but I am talking about Christ and the church. 33 However, each one of you also must love his wife as he loves himself, and the wife must respect her husband.

Comment by Diane on August 22, 2020

With birth control, the primary purpose of marriage has ceased to be reproductive for many couples. I would agree that two-parent homes generally offer greater stability than single parent homes. Plenty of men and women have been raised in homes where the adults are of the same sex (grandmother, mother) and they turn out just fine. Children thrive in homes with routines, responsibility, love, care, and generous amounts of quality time by the adults in their lives. It's interesting to ask a class of kindergartners about their evening bedtime routines. Almost to a child, those who have an established routine are more successful than those who don't. Doesn't mean those who don't aren't loved. Good parenting offers children security within a structured, loving environment with expectations, responsibility, praise, listening, reflection and encouragement.

What makes one happy in life and marriage may not be a recipe for happiness for another. To each their own.

Comment by Steve on August 22, 2020

Yes, for many people, marriage is non-reproductive. This is only new thing about it is how prevalent it has become. I heard a new term recently: "breeders", meant to be an insult to people that are in reproductive relationships. One can say to each their own, but there are consequences to a non-reproductive approach, namely, a species, society or country not being perpetuated. After fighting WWII, our country turned to replenishing the population, resulting in the baby boom. Large families well in excess of two children were common. These children were valued as being our future, a precious resource. Now, the powers that be seem to see the world as overpopulated and needing pruning. Oddly enough it is the developed west that has ended up getting pruned through the encouragement of non-reproductive relationships. As a result, those countries have relied upon immigration to maintain their populations. Of course, immigrants, assuming they absorb their host country's culture, will presumably also adopt a non-reproductive lifestyle. In this way America has become a kind of cultural black hole, where cultures arrive only to be extinguished even as they achieve more material success. One place where we don't see this dynamic: China, which is a rapidly rising powerhouse in large part because of its cohesive and huge population of (if I'm not mistaken) 1.6 billion. I note that China recently got rid of its one child per family rule.

Comment by Diane on August 23, 2020

People choose to have children – or not – for personal reasons. I married a Type 1 diabetic, a genetic condition that ran in his family. He died at the age of 45. He definitely did not want biological children and we talked about that before marriage, agreeing to adopt. We eventually had to choose not having children through adoption, as I was diagnosed with a chronic condition during the first few years of marriage. I suffered with tremendous fatigue yet needed to continue teaching. My job came with good health insurance for both of us, his didn't. He was also a melanoma cancer survivor, having had major surgery at age 19, before I met him. Would I have liked to have had children? Yes – but it just wasn't possible.

On the other hand, I have a dear friend who wanted a life companion and a family. He envied seeing couples walking hand in hand. He happened to be gay. He yearned for what others had and explored the possibility of marrying a woman – knowingly lying to her (he was absolutely not in the least attracted to women) to do so. He'd been raised by wonderful parents and loved being part of his church family that he was brought up in. He could not bring himself to be dishonest (some gay folks do conceal their identity, marrying someone of the opposite sex. Many such marriages end in divorce, leaving children and an unsuspecting straight spouse hurting (many such couples work at remaining supportive friends and loving parents, but still, there's pain). So my friend finally met someone he loved and married – another man. They adopted four children, all siblings from a family where the kids' heterosexual parents lost custody because they neglected and abused the children. Extended family members were not financially able to take the children. So my friend and his husband are raising them, but weekly take the kids for visits and family time with their biological family. They recognize the importance of maintaining family ties, the need for these kids to have stability, to be cared for and loved as a unit rather than split up in foster or separate adoptive homes. So, my friend and his husband aren't reproducing (with a surrogate, they could do so, however) – they took in four kids from straight parents. So, I'm not worried about a dismissing population due to reproductive choices. Most folks want children, but not all. Economics probably keeps people from having children – we need to, as a country, to be more supportive of families with children. Costs a lot to raise a child and in this day and age, I don't know how parents do it.

This discussion started out about Young Life. As a teacher, now retired, I was fiercely protective of my students. Their parents entrusted them to my care. I don't like Young Life's proselytizing strategy of targeting schools, becoming familiar with school kids without parents' knowledge or permission. Young Life volunteers may have the best of intentions while they volunteer in schools, show up at sports events, etc., but parents have a need to know their kids are not going to be intruded upon by adults with a religious or any other agenda. while their children are at school. There are other ways to proselytize that allow parents to responsibly have both knowledge and a say in their children's' extracurricular activities. Just my two cents (btw, my students' parents knew my open-door classroom policy – they could observe at any time without an appointment. Parents are rightfully concerned about teaching methods, classroom environment and making sure the teacher is teaching the state-prescribed curriculum and not something else).

Comment by Steve on August 23, 2020 at 11:18 am
Sounds you've have had your challenges and done the best you could do. I respect your willingness to share these aspects of your life. Given the amount of posting you do, I've often wondered if there wasn't an interesting origin story (like they say in the comics).

We'll have to disagree on being concerned about birthrates. There are many possible reasons the mainlines are dying, but a common reason given is low birthrates. In fact an Episcopal bishop (Schori) famously approved of the low birthrates in an interview, saying that Episcopalians don't take "more than their portion". One recent sarcastic article had Bishop Curry saying that having children was the worst thing an Episcopalian could do.

As regards Young Life personally, high school was a long time ago for me, but I remember there being flyers; if I was personally solicited, I don't remember it.

(Somebody would leave Chick comics around too.) It was obvious to me that it was a Christian group, and I knew what Christianity was, having been raised Episcopalian. I didn't look into it further; having attended church for all my childhood, I was ready for a break.

Comment by Diane on August 23, 2020 at 3:33 pm
I wonder if birthrates might go up if we gave more support to families. While I don't have children, I don't mind paying taxes to offer that support. Faith communities can't do it all. I was once a kid, too."

Article URL: https://juicyecumenism.com/2020/08/14/young-life-lgbt/

End

These particular exchanges of opinion of gay vs. straight youth on a Christian website are very interesting in that it follows a pattern of a typical reaction by the LBGTQI militants is to change and control the organization they belong to and disagree with, rather than start a new organization of like-minded LBGTQI youth.

7 - PROPAGANDA CAMPAIGN IN AMERICA'S MEDIA

The next article is perhaps the most stunning for its importance in the new formation of new strategy for homosexuals to gain acceptance. It is an excerpt from what became the playbook of the gay organizations on how to gain acceptance of their behavior in America. in a twist of who is doing what in the title itself. *"How America will conquer its fear and hatred of Gays in the 90s"* It became a best seller and is now out of print. It reminds me of my bi-sexual rector, who was married, who once said to me in a meeting, "This is my lifestyle. I am comfortable with it and I have no problem with it. You are the problem, Brad, for you won't accept it." I was stunned in that declaration.

The Homosexual Propaganda Campaign in America's Media

www.truthaccordingtoscripture.com

"The powerful, sophisticated psychological techniques that the homosexual movement has used to manipulate the public is the media."

Introduction

If you think that the radical changes in the minds of Americans — and in your own mind — about homosexuality in the last decade are an accident, you must read the section below. From the 1989 book, "After the Ball - How America will conquer its fear and hatred of Gays in the 90s" (Penguin Books) which immediately became a beacon for the then-emerging homosexual movement.

Building on the basic strategies outlined in Marshall Kirk's groundbreaking 1987 article, "The Overhauling of Straight America", this book puts forth the very sophisticated psychological persuasion and propaganda mass media techniques that we've all seen and been affected by over the years—but never understood what was happening.

Kirk is a researcher in neuropsychiatry. The book describes his co-author Hunter Madsen as having received a doctorate in Politics from Harvard in 1985 and an expert on public persuasion tactics and social marketing, who has designed commercial advertising on Madison Avenue and served as a consultant to gay media campaigns across the country and appears frequently on national media as an advocate for gay rights.

A founding work of the modern homosexual movement, this book covers a wide discussion of tactics and observations relating to the homosexual movement. But the overall main psychological strategies are well summarized in a ten-page section (pp. 147-157) titled "Pushing the right buttons: halting, derailing, or reversing the 'engine of prejudice'". Reprinted below, this is the meat of the book which has been re-used and referred to by the homosexual movement countless times.

It discusses (1) Desensitization, (2) Jamming, and (3) Conversion.

Of particular note is their tactical device throughout the book of referring to religious dissenters and other critics of homosexual behavior as "bigots." Their language is purposefully crude to enhance that idea. Much like the "big lie" theory developed in the 1920s and 1930s by the Nazis, the constant repetition of this eventually has the desired psychological effect on masses of people.

As you read this, keep in mind that it was written in 1989 -- and look around to see how far the homosexual movement has gotten using these techniques.

Pushing the Right Buttons: Halting, Derailing, or Reversing the Engine of Prejudice

From "After the Ball - How America will conquer its fear and hatred of Gays in the 90s."

Penguin Books, 1989 pp. 147-157.

by Marshall K. Kirk and Hunter Madsen

In the past, gays have tinkered ineptly with the engine of prejudice. Is it possible to tinker more favorably? We present (in order of increasing vigor and desirability) three general approaches [which are vastly better than what we've tried in the past].

These approaches, once understood, will lead us directly to the principles upon which a viable campaign can be erected.

I. Desensitization
From the point of view of evolution, prejudice is an alerting signal, warning tribal mammals that a potentially dangerous alien mammal is in the vicinity, and should be fought or fled. Alerting mechanisms respond to novelties in the environment, because novelties represent change from the usual, and are, therefore, potentially important.

One of two things can happen: (1) If the alerting mechanism is very strongly activated, it will produce an unendurable emotional state, forcing the tribal mammal to fight the novelty or flee it. (2) If, however, the novelty is either low-grade, or simply odd without being threatening, the alerting mechanism will be mildly activated, producing an emotional state that, if other environmental circumstances militate against it, will be too weak to motivate any actual behavioral response. In the latter case, the mammal may peer curiously at the novelty for quite some time, but will not do anything about it, or to it.

As a general physio-psychological rule, novelties cease to be novel if they just stick around long enough; they also cease to activate alerting mechanisms. There are excellent evolutionary reasons for this: if the mammal either has no good reason to respond, or is for some reason incapable of doing so, it is actually hindered in its normal activities if its attention continues to be taken up by an irrelevancy. You'll have noted this in your own life: if you hear a protracted, earsplitting mechanical screech, you'll either be so alarmed, or so annoyed, that you'll be forced to take action; if you hear a softer--though, perhaps, nonetheless annoying--sound, like the ticking of a clock, and can't shut it off, you will, eventually, shut it out, and may cease to hear it altogether. Similarly with a rank odor, smelled upon entering a room; if you can't get rid of it, you eventually cease to smell it.

Franz Kafka wrote a delightful fable ("The Animal in the Synagogue") that might almost have had Desensitization in mind. His story--never finished-deals with a peculiar animal, the only one of its kind, which has been living, since time immemorial, in a synagogue. The elders take a dim view of this state of affairs; though quiet, the animal emerges from its nook during services and distracts the women (who sit at the back) from their devotions. Moreover, there is no telling, with so very odd an animal, what its habits might eventually prove to be. Suppose it bites? There is talk of mounting an expedition to catch and kill it. But the synagogue is very large and very old, with a thousand bolt- holes in which the animal might hide, and it is capable of climbing high and running fast. Any such expedition would be difficult, and would run the risk not only of failure, but of damaging irreplaceable artwork. The upshot is that the elders call the whole thing off; and, as the animal never gives anyone the least trouble, they get used to its presence, and eventually cease to think about it at all.

Apply this to the problem of homohatred. If gays present themselves-- or allow themselves to be presented--as overwhelmingly different and threatening, they will put straights on a triple-red alert, driving them to overt acts of political oppression or physical violence. If, however, gays can live alongside straights, visibly but as inoffensively as possible, they will arouse a low-grade alert only, which, though annoying to straights, will eventually diminish for purely physiological reasons. Straights will be desensitized. Put more simply, if you go out of your way to be unendurable, people will try to destroy you; otherwise, they might eventually get used to you. This commonsense axiom should make it clear that living down to the stereotype, a la Gender-Bending, is a very bad idea.

We can extract the following principle for our campaign to desensitize straights to gays and gayness, inundate them in a continuous flood of gay-related advertising, presented in the least offensive fashion possible. If straights can't shut off the shower, they may at least eventually get used to being wet.

Of course, while sheer indifference is, itself, vastly preferable to hatred and threats, we would like to do better than that. We turn next to more difficult, but also more vigorous and rewarding, tactics.

2. Jamming
The engine of prejudice can be made to grind to a halt not only by Desensitization, in which it is simply allowed to run out of steam, but also by the more active process of Jamming. As the name implies, Jamming involves the insertion into the engine of a pre-existing, incompatible emotional response, gridlocking its mechanism as thoroughly as though one had sprinkled fine sand into the workings of an old-fashioned pocket watch. Jamming, as an approach, is more active and aggressive than Desensitization; by the same token, it is also more enjoyable and heartening.

Jamming makes use of the rules of Associative Conditioning (the psychological process whereby, when two things are repeatedly juxtaposed, one's feelings about one thing are transferred to the other) and Direct Emotional Modeling (the inborn tendency of human beings to feel what they perceive others to be feeling).

Turning Associative Conditioning and Direct Emotional Modeling against themselves, we Jam by forging a fresh link between, on the one hand, some part of the mechanism, and, on the other, a pre-existing, external, opposed, and therefore incompatible emotional response. Ideally, the bigot subjected to such counterconditioning will ultimately experience two emotional responses to the hated object, opposed and competing. The consequent internal confusion has two effects: first, it is unpleasant-- we can call it 'emotional dissonance,' after Festinger--and will tend to result in an alteration of previous beliefs and feelings so as to resolve the internal conflict. Since the weaker of the clashing emotional associations is the more likely to give way, we can achieve optimal results by linking the prejudicial response to a stronger and more fundamental structure of belief and emotion. (Naturally, in some people this will be impossible, as prejudicial hatred is the strongest) element in their beliefs, emotions, and motivations. Without resorting to prefrontal lobotomy--ah! sweet dreams!--these people are more or less unsalvageable.) Second, even where an optimal resolution does not occur, the internal dissonance will tend to inhibit overt expression of the prejudicial emotion--which is, in itself, useful and relieving.

The 'incompatible emotional response' is directed primarily against the emotional rewards of prejudicial solidarity. All normal people feel shame when they perceive that they are not thinking, feeling, or acting like one of the pack. And, these days, all but the stupidest and most unregenerate of bigots perceive that prejudice against all other minority groups-e.g., blacks, Jews, Catholics, women, et al.--has long since ceased to be approved, let alone fashionable, and that to express such prejudices, if not to hold them, makes one decidedly not one of the pack. It was permissible, some forty years ago, to tell the vilest ethnic jokes at the average party, and, if the joke were reasonably well told, the joker could expect to receive applause and approval from his or her roistering confreres. (Should you find this hard to believe, read 2500 Jokes for All Occasions, a popular 1942 compilation by Powers Moulton, which will surely stand your hair on end.) With the exception of certain benighted social classes and backward areas of the country, this is quite generally no longer the case.

The trick is to get the bigot into the position of feeling a conflicting twinge of shame, along with his reward, whenever his homohatred surfaces, so that his reward will be diluted or spoiled. This can be accomplished in a variety of ways, all making use of repeated exposure to pictorial images or verbal statements that are incompatible with his self-image as a well-liked person, one who fits in with the rest of the crowd. Thus, propagandistic advertisement can depict homophobic and homohating bigots as crude loudmouths and assholes--people who say not only 'faggot' but 'nigger,' 'kike,' and other shameful epithets--who are 'not Christian.' It can show them being criticized, hated, shunned. It can depict gays experiencing horrific suffering as the direct result of homohatred-suffering of which even most bigots would be ashamed to be the cause. It can, in short, link homohating bigotry with all sorts of attributes the bigot would be ashamed to possess, and with social consequences he would find unpleasant and scary. The attack, therefore, is on self-image and on the pleasure in hating.

When our ads show a bigot--just like the members of the target audience--being criticized, hated, and shunned, we make use of Direct Emotional Modeling as well. Remember, a bigot seeks approval and liking from 'his crowd.' When he sees someone like himself being disapproved of and disliked by ordinary Joes, Direct Emotional Modeling ensures that he will feel just what they feel -- and transfer it to himself. This wrinkle effectively elicits shame and doubt, Jamming any pleasure he might normally feel. In a very real sense, every time a bigot sees such a thing, he is un- learning a little bit of the lesson of prejudice taught him by his parents and peers.

Such an approach may seem much too weak to work, yet bear these thoughts in mind: (a) the procedure is exactly that which formed the prejudicial complex to begin with; (b) the majority of casual bigots do not, in fact, see themselves as unpleasant people and would hate to think that others see them as such, let alone that their hatred has caused suffering and death; (c) there has, in fact, been a major turnaround in the acceptability, in this country, of prejudice against other minority groups, due, in our opinion, in no small part to exactly such counterconditioning and linking; and (d) such an approach has actually been used in TV advertisements, most memorably in an antidrinking ad showing a teenage boy drinking at a party, but not meeting with approval: indeed, as he gets more and more drunk, his behavior becomes more and more obnoxious, and he is regarded by the other partiers with disgust; ultimately, his head turns into that of a heehawing jackass. One can readily see how this sort of thing could be adapted to our own purposes.

Note that the bigot need not actually be made to believe that he is such a heinous creature, that others will now despise him, and that he has been the immoral agent of suffering. It would be impossible to make him believe any such thing. Rather, our effect is achieved without reference to facts, logic, or proof. Just as the bigot became such, without any say in the matter, through repeated infralogical emotional conditioning, his bigotry can be alloyed in exactly the same way, whether he is conscious of the attack or not. Indeed, the more he is distracted by any incidental, even specious, surface arguments, the less conscious he'll be of the true nature of the process--which is all to the good.

In short, Jamming succeeds insofar as it inserts even a slight frisson of doubt and shame into the previously unalloyed, self- righteous pleasure. The approach can be quite useful and effective -- if our message can get the massive exposure upon which all else depends.

3.Conversion
Desensitization aims at lowering the intensity of antigay emotional reactions to a level approximating sheer indifference; Jamming attempts to blockade or counteract the rewarding 'pride in prejudice' (peace, Jane Austen!) by attaching to homohatred a pre-existing, and punishing, sense of shame in being a bigot, a horse's ass, and a beater and murderer. Both Desensitization and Jamming, though extremely useful, are mere preludes to our highest --though necessarily very long-range--goal, which is Conversion.

It isn't enough that antigay bigots should become confused about us, or even indifferent to us--we are safest, in the long run, if we can actually make them like us. Conversion aims at just this.

Please don't confuse Conversion with political Subversion. The word 'subversion' has a nasty ring, of which the American people are inordinately afraid--and on their guard against. Yet, ironically, by Conversion we actually mean something far more profoundly threatening to the American Way of Life, without which no truly sweeping social change can occur. We mean conversion of the average American's emotions, mind, and will, through a planned psychological attack, in the form of propaganda fed to the nation via the media. We mean 'subverting' the mechanism of prejudice to our own ends--using the very processes that made America hate us to turn their hatred into warm regard--whether they like it or not.

Put briefly, if Desensitization lets the watch run down, and Jamming throws sand in the works, Conversion reverses the spring so that the hands run backward.

Conversion makes use of Associative Conditioning, much as Jamming does--indeed, in practice the two processes overlap-- but far more ambitiously. In Conversion, the bigot, who holds a very negative stereotypic picture, is repeatedly exposed to literal picture/label pairs, in magazines, and on billboards and TV, of gay-explicitly labeled as such!--who not only don't look like his picture of a homosexual but are carefully selected to look either like the bigot and his friends, or like any one of his other stereotypes of all-right guys-- the kind of people he already likes and ` admires. This image must, of necessity, be carefully tailored to be free of absolutely every element of the widely held stereotypes of how 'faggots' look, dress, and sound. He--or she--must not be too well or fashionably dressed; must not be too handsome--that is, mustn't look like a model--or well groomed. The image must be that of an icon of normality--a good beginning would be to take a long look at Coors beer and Three Musketeers candy commercials. Subsequent ads can branch out from that solid basis to include really adorable, athletic teenagers, kindly grandmothers, avuncular policemen, ad infinitem.

The objection will be raised--and raised and raised--that we would 'Uncle Tommify' the gay community; that we are exchanging one false stereotype for another equally false; that our ads are lies; that that is not how all gays actually look; that gays know it, and bigots know it. Yes, of course--we know it, too. But it makes no difference that the ads are lies; not to us, because we're using them to ethically good effect, to counter negative stereotypes that are every bit as much lies, and far more wicked ones; not to bigots, because the ads will have their effect on them whether they believe them or not.

When a bigot is presented with an image of the sort of person of whom he already has a positive stereotype, he experiences an involuntary rush of positive emotion, of good feeling; he's been conditioned to experience it. But, here, the good picture has the bad label--gay! (The ad may say something rather like 'Beauregard Smith--beer drinker, Good Ole Boy, pillar of the community, 100%

American, and gay as a mongoose.') The bigot will feel two incompatible emotions: a good response to the picture, a bad response to the label. At worst, the two will cancel one another, and we will have successfully jammed, as above. At best, Associative Conditioning will, to however small an extent, transfer the positive emotion associated with the picture to the label itself, not immediately replacing the negative response, but definitely weakening it.

You may wonder why the transfer wouldn't proceed in the opposite direction. The reason is simple: pictures are stronger than words and evoke emotional responses more powerfully. The bigot is presented with an actual picture; its label will evoke in his mind his own stereotypic picture, but what he sees in his mind's eye will be weaker than what he actually sees in front of him with the eyes in his face. The more carefully selected the advertised image is to reflect his ideal of the sort of person who just couldn't be gay, the more effective it will be. Moreover, he will, by virtue of logical necessity, see the positive picture in the ad before it can arouse his negative 'picture,' and first impressions have an advantage over second.

In Conversion, we mimic the natural process of stereotype- learning, with the following effect: we take the bigot's good feelings about all-right guys, and attach them to the label 'gay,' either weakening or, eventually, replacing his bad feelings toward the label and the prior stereotype.

Understanding Direct Emotional Modeling, you'll readily foresee its application to Conversion: whereas in Jamming the target is shown a bigot being rejected by his crowd for his prejudice against gays, in Conversion the target is shown his crowd actually associating with gays in good fellowship. Once again, it's very difficult for the average person, who, by nature and training, almost invariably feels what he sees his fellows feeling, not to re-spend in this knee-jerk fashion to a sufficiently calculated advertisement. In a way, most advertisement is founded upon an answer of Yes, definitely! to Mother's sarcastic question: I suppose if all the other kids jumped off a bridge and killed themselves, you would, too?

72

We've now outlined three major modes by which we can alter the itinerary of the engine of prejudice in our favor. Desensitization lets the engine run out of steam, causing it to halt on the tracks indefinitely. Jamming, in essence, derails it. Conversion-- our ambitious long-range goal--puts the engine into reverse gear and sends it back whence it came.

These modes are abstract--we've only hinted, here and there, at how they can be harnessed and put to work for us in a practical propaganda campaign . . .

Our goal, being high, is also difficult. The bottleneck in reaching it, however, isn't lack of knowledge of the psychological principles. Involved, nor lack of efficacy in the methods available; the principles are known, and the methods work. The bottleneck is purely and simply achieving a sufficient scope for the dissemination of our propaganda. Success depends, as always, on flooding the media. And that, in turn, means money, which means man-hours, which means unifying the gay community for a concerted effort. Let's be blunt: those who aren't with us in this effort, either because they have better ways of wasting their time, or because they think we're politically incorrect, are most decidedly against us, against unification, and against the best interests of the gay community as a whole.

End

Truth According to Scripture Editor's Note: Keep in mind this article was published in 1987. Since that time homosexual activists have made remarkable progress in their media campaign. There are over 25 openly "gay" characters on TV shows such as, Roseanne, Melrose Place, Picket Fences, Northern Exposure, Ellen, Dawson's Creek, Will and Grace, etc. where homosexuality is presented as normal, natural behavior on a regular basis. NBC News did a three-day series on "Gays in America" in September that had no opposing view, other than one brief statement by Dr. Paul Cameron. There's a proliferation of "gay" propaganda being shoved down our throats in movies like "The Crying Game", "Philadelphia", "Priscilla, Queen of the Desert", "Go Fish", and many more.

"... Hollywood is coming out of the closet, and homosexual activists are jumping up and down for joy."

Hollywood is indeed coming, out of the closet, and homosexual activists are jumping up and down for joy. Why? Because they know Americans flock to the movie theaters in droves, and that gradually the message of accepting homosexuality as a normal variant of human sexuality is getting through to people-minds are being changed.

Two years after "The Overhauling of Straight America" appeared, the book, "*After the Ball—How America will conquer its fear and hatred of Gays in the 1990's*", by Marshall Kirk and Hunter Madsen, was published. *After the Ball* expanded on these ideas, largely from the standpoint of psychological manipulation and persuasion tactics of Americans toward the homosexual cause, complete with sample print ads to use, as well as suggestions for radio and TV spots.

For those of you who want to investigate more about the homosexual agenda and various strategies I recommend the book *After the Ball* by Kirk and Madsen. (Check your library first; I hate to see these guys make money to support their cause.) Both authors are Harvard grads—Kirk is a researcher in neuropsychiatry, while Madsen is "an expert on public persuasion tactics and social marketing." The book is an expansion of the above article complete with sample print ads to use, as well as suggestions for radio, TV spots.

NOTE: In accordance with Title 17 U.S.C. section 107, this material is reproduced for non-profit educational purposes only. For more information go to: https://www.law.cornell.edu/uscode/17/107.shtml

[1] From "After the Ball - How America will conquer its fear and hatred of Gays in the 90s." Penguin Books, 1989 pp. 147-157.

https://www.truthaccordingtoscripture.com/documents/politics/homosexual-agenda-ball.php#.X_d6--hKgv4

End

Let there be light, Lord.

8 - INDOCTRINATING CHILDREN THROUGH PUBLIC LIBRARIES

What you need to know about the "Drag Queen" indoctrination of children in your public libraries: Where it comes from and how they make it happen.

MassResistance.org   October 24, 2019 [1]

When people in a community find out that their local public library is hosting a "Drag Queen Story Hour" – bizarre men in garish women's clothes reading LGBT-themed books to young children ages 3-8 – their first reaction is usually shock and disgust. They wonder, "How is this happening?"

Then they ask, "How can this insane thing be stopped?" Little do they know that by that time, virtually everything is already stacked against them. At every move, the supporting local officials, politicians, and even the library rules seem impenetrable, and the opposing citizens get nowhere.

So what is really going on?
Much has already been written about how hideous and destructive this program is for young children, and how the "Drag Queens" are overwhelmingly open sexual deviants (and brag about on social media), if not actual convicted sex offenders.

In the larger sense, this is the latest extension of the LGBT movement's obsession with children, which in recent years has reached first into high schools, then into middle schools, and lately into the elementary schools. The younger they get them, the more strongly embedded will be their sick messages, they believe.

It starts with the local library staff

The library profession tends to attract very radical, pro-LGBT, social-justice types of people. We're not sure why, but it's clearly true. Many of these people have no children of their own and don't see the world as most parents of young children do. Furthermore, in most areas the library officials have developed a strong influence on who sits on the local Library Boards which oversee them and are thus generally populated with like-minded people.

Thus, the library staff sees no problem at all with these "Drag Queens" and probably feel quite positive about them being around children. Most parents don't appreciate how perverse and abnormal this situation is.

The national "Drag Queen Story Hour" organization

How are the "Drag Queens" recruited from their sexual underworld, then set up in these slickly promoted library events across the country with a list of books to read? The national Drag Queen Story Hour (DQSH) group appears to be the organizational muscle behind that. Their website boasts 47 local chapters across America (including a few overseas) and there are probably more than that.

The DQSH movement started in 2015 in San Francisco. But it now appears to be run out of, or in conjunction with, the Brooklyn, NY Public Library.

LGBT-themed books for the Drag Queens to read to children. The Brooklyn Public Library has put together two lists, one for toddlers and preschoolers, and one for elementary school children. While there are a few innocuous titles (such as The Very Hungry Caterpillar), most push LGBTQ ideology. (The reader can take even an innocuous book and give it an LGBTQ twist.)

Here's a sampling of the books: (We've included a few other titles from news stories on DQSH events around the country.)

Boys wearing girls' clothes or wanting to play with dolls: Sparkle Boy, Jacob's New Dress, My Princess Boy, Morris Micklewhite and the

Tangerine Dress, Julian Is a Mermaid, Teddy's Favorite Toy, William's Doll, Clive and His Babies, Just Add Glitter

"Gender" – "identity" – "transitioning": I Am Jazz, Born Bad, I'm a Girl, Neither, It's OK to Be Different, Be Who You Are, A Color of His Own, I Like Myself, Where Is the Green Sheep?, Introducing Teddy, A Crayon's Story, Not Every Princess, Leonardo the Terrible Monster, Froodle

LGBT Families: And Tango Makes Three, Worm Loves Worm, Families!, Stella Brings the Family, A family is a family is a family, Antonio's Card, The Family Book, Love Makes a Family, Willow at the Wedding

Pride: This day in June

Feminist: Tattherhood – Feminist Folktales, Goddess Girls – Echo the Copycat, Not All Princesses Dress in Pink, Clever Manka, Tutus Aren't My Style

The DQSH organization also publishes its own material for children such as The Dragtivity Book to "help adults and kids explore drag, gender, and identity together." DQSH collaborated on the book with the drag queen enterprise, SezMe.me. That group's website has disturbing videos with little children alongside creepy drag queens, talking about trans pronoun usage and gender fluidity.

Given the ideological makeup of library staffs, it's probably not a hard sell to get these programs into the local libraries around the country.

There is no question that the purpose of these programs is to push these perverse sexual issues into the minds of children. How does this affect children? The library staffs obviously don't seem to care.

Making it happen: The American Library Association
These "programs" are usually so bizarre and so shocking to a community that the local library staff needs well thought-out tactics and strategies for successfully steamrolling everyone who might be an obstacle – including members of the public, the media, public officials, or even other staffers. This is where the American Library Association (ALA) comes in. In fact, the ALA is clearly the most

powerful force in this whole process.

Most people think of the ALA as a rather boring professional association. Nothing could be further from the truth. It is an intensely radical organization that has a strong alliance with the national LGBT movement. Folks were given a taste of that recently when The Federalist published this shocking article about the ALA's annual conference.

The ALA website is veritable armory of articles and resources for library staff members and LGBT activists to make sure that nothing gets in the way of Drag Queen events in any public library anywhere. Thanks to a recent report at LifeSiteNews many of these have been brought to light:

#LibrariesRespond Campaign. A real education! Created by the ALA to answer the backlash over DQSHs and Drag 101 events. Provides policy materials and resources to "defend pride at the local library."

Responding to and preparing for controversial events and speakers. How to make sure controversial speakers and programs aren't successfully challenged or stopped by members of the community.

How to be a "secret librarian advocate operative." To help librarians promote acceptance of the LBGTQ lifestyle in resistant communities, the ALA published a disgusting blog post by a library staffer in Maryland.

Gay, Lesbian, Bisexual, Transgender Roundtable. Provides tools and resources to promote acceptance of the LGBTQ lifestyle through the American library system and recommends reading lists for libraries with "significant gay, lesbian, bisexual, transgender, or queer/questioning content, aimed at children and youth from birth to age 18." ...

ALA Office of Diversity, Literacy, and Outreach Services. Helps library staff deal with pushback when implementing "social justice" and LGBT materials in the library.

Freedom to Read Foundation. Supported by the ALA. Funds

litigation when necessary and so-called "Banned Books Week" education.

Office for Intellectual Freedom. Helps library staff and left-wing activists fight pro-family people who want to remove graphic sexual children's books.

Intellectual Freedom Committee. Information for staff on: "Access to Library Resources and Services Regardless of Sex, Gender Identity, Gender Expression, or Sexual Orientation: An Interpretation of the Library Bill of Rights."

This is what parents across the country are up against when "Drag Queens" come to their library to target young children.

Local LGBT activists keeping the pressure on

As mentioned above, being able to "connect" with children is an obsession of the LGBT movement. Once the DQSH events are in place, local LGBT activists (including Antifa groups, whose members appear to have sexual issues) energetically mobilize to confront faltering political leaders or parents who rise up to oppose it. As a result, one sees a disturbing cave-in among public officials.

Pro-LGBT activists from around the region will come and bring children to these events to make it appear popular. But one rarely, if ever, sees local parents there who are not part of that movement.

What can you do?

As bad as this may seem, there are effective counter-tactics and strategies that can be successfully used. The ALA, LGBT activists, and the local library staffs depend on parents being ignorant, somewhat frightened, and isolated. As our readers have seen, it's not easy, but Mass Resistance organizes and mobilizes parents in a community to take on this fight in a way that puts the opposition off balance and can lead to victory – as well as sending a clear message to the public officials about future activity they might consider.

Secondly, EVERY city, town, and school system should stop paying the ALA dues for its library employees. These dues are fairly expensive and serve to fund nothing but destructive behavior.

Third, thanks largely to the ALA, these books are on local library shelves everywhere in the country, whether or not there's a DQSH planned! Community members need to push to get this harmful LGBT propaganda out of the children's sections of the public library. Yes: These books should be banned!

And finally, whenever these kinds of radical programs or materials pushed in a public library, this is a clear message that the community needs to take strong steps to remove the library staff responsible as well as the governing Library Board members. They need to understand what their role is – and isn't!

https://www.massresistance.org/docs/gen3/19d/ALA-push-behind-DQSH/index.html

End

Let there be Light Lord.

9 THE RAINBOW BOOK LIST

I never imagined such a thing as the Rainbow Book List even existed before I did my research for this book. More amazing is the fact that The American Library Association has committees like the Rainbow Round Table and Social Responsibilities Round Table to stay current on books that address these issues. This is another example of the strategy of gay organizations to infiltrate American culture and normalize their behavior. Through associations like the American Library Association they work to reach children and young adults so they can normalize their behavior as if there is no other behavior, and there is no controversy.

The Rainbow Book List

The Rainbow Book List is created by the Rainbow Book List Committee of the Rainbow Round Table of the American Library Association. Originally a joint project between the Rainbow Round Table (formerly Gay, Lesbian, Bisexual, and Transgender Round Table) and the Social Responsibilities Round Table, the Rainbow Book List presents an annual bibliography of quality books with significant and authentic LGBQTIA+ content, which are recommended for people from birth through eighteen years of age. [1]

The committee is proud to announce the 2020 Rainbow Book List. The list is a curated bibliography highlighting books with significant gay, lesbian, bisexual, transgender, or queer/questioning content, aimed at children and youth from birth to age 18. This list is intended to aid youth and those working with youth in selecting high-quality books published in the United States of America between July 1, 2018 and December 31, 2019.

As a committee, we evaluated over 550 books and selected 92 titles. Starred titles indicate the Rainbow Book List's Top Ten choices, which are the books that the committee considers to be of exceptional merit.

This year, our committee has noticed an abundance of genre fiction, as well as books whose plots do not revolve around anxiety concerning a queer character's identity. Micro trends that we've noticed this year have been books about birds or with birds in the title, and books about queer witches. We've also seen an increase in books with non-binary, asexual-spectrum, and bisexual characters.

Now, without further ado, we present to you the 2020 Rainbow Book List!

Picture Book Non-Fiction

Little Bee Books, ed. Our Rainbow. 2019. 20p. Little Bee Books. $8.99 (9781499809343). Ages 2-5. Through page spreads by different illustrators, Our Rainbow explores the traditional meanings assigned to each of the colors on the rainbow pride flag.

Meltzer, Brad, and Christopher Eliopoulos. I am Billie Jean King. 2019. 40p. Penguin/Dial Books for Young Readers, $15.99. Ages 5-8. (9780735228740). The engaging story of tennis star Billy Jean King and her work, both on and off the court, to become a sports icon and women's rights activist – as well as King's realization that she is gay. Includes timeline and photographs.

Pierets, Fleur, and Fatinha Ramos. Love Around the World. 2019. 40p. Six Foot Press. $18.95 (9781644420058). Ages 4-8. Fleur and her wife Julian are on an adventure to get married in every country that legally allows same-sex marriage. The couple learns about a variety of wedding traditions that they incorporate in each place they wed.

*Sanders, Rob, and Jamey Christoph. Stonewall: A Building. An Uprising. A Revolution. 2019. 40p. Random House Children's Books. $17.99 (9781524719524). Ages 5-9. The historic Stonewall Inn narrates its own history as well as the subsequent 1969 uprising. Includes a short essay about the Stonewall Inn, photographs, interview with activist Martin Boyce, glossary, and a bibliography.

Stevenson, Robin. Pride Colors. 2019. 28p. Orca, $9.95

(9781459820708). Ages 0-4. "A bright red heart, a little star. I love you just the way you are." This gentle book alternates pages that focuses on each color of the rainbow with touching, affirming messages for any parent or caregiver to share with their child.

Thorn, Theresa and Noah Grigni. It Feels Good to Be Yourself: A Book About Gender Identity. 2019. 40p. Macmillan/Henry Holt and Company. $17.99 (9781250302953). Ages 3-6. Colorful illustrations and simple language explain the basics of gender identity and cis, trans, and nonbinary genders. An affirming and uncomplicated introduction to gender concepts for all children from an own voices nonbinary author.

Picture Book Fiction

Gale, Heather, and Mika Song. Ho'onani : Hula Warrior. 2019. 40p. Penguin/Tundra Books, $17.99 (9780735264496). Ages 4-7. Based on a true story, this book follows Ho'onani as she takes on a traditional boys-only role in a hula performance at school. Ho'onani asserts herself as existing in the middle between genders.

Haack, Daniel, Isabel Galupa, and Becca Human. Maiden and Princess. 2019. 40p. Little Bee Books. $17.99 (9781499807769). Ages 4-8. A warrior maiden begrudgingly attends the matchmaker ball at the request of her friend, the Prince. She does end up finding true love — with his sister, the Princess.

Hoffman, Sarah, Ian Hoffman, and Chris Case. Jacob's Room to Choose. 2019. 32p. American Psychological Association/Magination Press, $17.99 (9781433830730). Ages 6-9. Jacob (of Jacob's New Dress) encounters hostility when using the school bathroom. In response, their teacher helps the students see that people do not always conform to strict gender presentations. Together as a class, they create improved signs for the bathrooms.

*Lukoff, Kyle and Kaylani Juanita. When Aidan Became a Brother. 2019. 32p. Lee & Low Books. $18.95 (9781620148372). Ages 4-8. This heartwarming picture book from an own voices trans author and an own voices illustrator of color explores what it's like for Aidan when his parents expect a new baby. He wants to ensure everything will be just right for his younger sibling. Aidan knows that sometimes grown-ups can make mistakes, like when his parents thought he was a girl when he was born. As Aidan prepares for his role as big brother, he realizes that mistakes can be fixed with open communication.

Phi, Bao and Basia Tran. My Footprints. 2019. 32p. Capstone, $19.99 (9781684460007). Ages 5-9. Thuy is bullied at school because she has two mothers, and because of her heritage. This picture book from an own voices Vietnamese author shows how Thuy draws strength from her culture when she imagines her snowy footprints are those of wild animals.

*Smith, Heather and Brooke Kerrigan. A Plan for Pops. 2019. 32p. Orca Book Publishers. $19.95 (9781459816145). Ages 3-6. Saturdays are special for Lou and Lou's grandparents, Grandad and Pop. When Pop loses the ability to walk, he doesn't want to leave his room, but Lou comes up with a plan to help!

Juvenile Non-Fiction Branfman, Jonathan and Julie Benbassat. You Be You! The Kid's Guide to Gender, Sexuality, and Family. 2019. 80p. Jessica Kingsley Publishers. $18.95 (9781787750104). Ages 5-10. This simple book guides readers through the rainbow of gender and attraction spectrums, and breaks down common ideas about marriage, having kids, and even romance itself.

Medina, Nico and Jake Murray. What Was Stonewall? 2019. 112p. Penguin, $5.99 (9781524786007). Grades 3-6. Beginning with the 1969 Stonewall Riots, this book provides a broad overview of the LGBTQ+ rights movement, from the early days of bohemian Greenwich Village, to the dedication of the Stonewall National Monument in 2016. Plenty of photographs and illustrations make this accessible for middle grade readers interested in LGBTQ+ history.

Middle Grade Non-Fiction
Pitman, Gayle E and Fred Sargeant. The Stonewall Riots: Coming Out in the Streets. 2019. 224p. Abrams/Abrams Books for Young Readers, $17.99 (9781419737206). Grades 5-9. Pitman takes a uniquely archival approach to her subject, examining objects that provide insight into the Stonewall Riots, their social context, LGBT history, and the gay rights movement. Includes a timeline, notes, bibliography, and index.

Middle Grade Fiction

Bigelow, Lisa Jenn. Hazel's Theory of Evolution. 2019. 336p. HarperCollins, $16.99 (9780062791177). Grades 3-7. Realistic Fiction. Hazel would rather get lost in the pages of an encyclopedia than deal with the mounting changes in her life: starting over at a new school in her last year of middle school; worrying about her mom's pregnancy following two miscarriages; and questioning romantic attraction as other girls focus on boys.

Blake, Ashley Herring. The Mighty Heart of Sunny St. James. 2019.375p. Hachette/Little, Brown and Company, $16.99 (9780316515535). Ages 4-8. Realistic Fiction. After finally getting a heart transplant, Sunny's summer plan is to "do awesome amazing things she could never do before." On her quest to find a new best friend and kiss a boy, she wonders if she really wants to kiss a boy at all.

Bunker, Lisa. Zenobia July. 2019. 313p. Penguin/Viking Books for Young Readers, $17.99 (9780451479402). Grades 5+. Realistic Fiction. Zenobia has a whole lot of new in her life: a new school, new friends, a new place to live with her lesbian aunts, and a new opportunity to finally live as a girl. When someone posts hateful Islamophobic and transphobic memes on the school website, Zenobia knows her coding skills from her old life could help her catch the culprit, and suddenly she has new decisions to make: who can she trust? And is catching the hacker worth the attention and risk?

Diloway, Margaret. Summer of a Thousand Pies. 2019. 384p. HarperCollins/Balzer + Bray, $16.99 (9780062803467). Grades 3-6. Realistic Fiction. After her mother's death, Cady's father spirals into substance abuse which lands him in jail. Cady experiences neglect, food insecurity, homelessness, and the foster care system before she's sent to live with two aunts she has never met. Resistant at first, Cady soon discovers a passion for baking. But the perfect pie crust isn't the solution for everything; she must also deal with her trauma — and the realization that her parents were more flawed than she knew. Back matter contains recipes, including one for a gluten-free pie crust.

Holt, K. A. Redwood and Ponytail. 2019. 418p. Chronicle Books, $18.99 (9781452172880). Grades 5-8. Realistic Fiction/Verse Novel. At first, Kate and Tam dismiss each other as "just a cheerleader" and "just a jock." But as they spend more time together, they challenge the ways others have defined them and begin to define and accept themselves.

Pancholy, Maulik. The Best at It. 2019. 336p. HarperCollins/Balzer + Bray, $16.99 (9780062866417). Grades 5-7. Realistic Fiction. Rahul, a 7th grade Indian-American boy growing up in a small town, deals with anxiety, bullies, racial prejudice, and being different by following his grandfather's advice – find something to be the best at. As Rahul figures out who he is, his best friend Chelsea and his family are there to cheer him on, and he hopes that just maybe his crush Justin will start to notice him.

Salazar, Aida. The Moon Within. 2019. 240p. Scholastic/Arthur A. Levine Books, $17.99 (9781338283372). Grades 3-6. Realistic Fiction/Verse Novel. Celi is unhappy about her impending menstruation and even more unhappy that her mom wants to celebrate it in a reclaimed indigenous ceremony. What's more, her best friend is coming out as nonbinary and the boy she likes is being a jerk about it. Can Celi find the strength to both be true to herself and loyal to her friend?

Young Adult Non-Fiction
Baumann, Jason, ed. Love and Resistance. 2019. 224p. W. W. Norton & Company, Inc. $24.95 (9781324002062). Grades 10+. Drawn from The New York Public Library Archives, this collection of photographs by Kay Lahusen and Diana Davies documents LGBTQ+ activists and activism in the 1960s and 70s. Photographs are organized into four sections: Visibility, Love, Pride, and Protest, and each section is contextualized in a brief introduction; individual photographs are also described and contextualized.

Bausum, Ann. Viral: the Fight against AIDS in America. 2019. 176p. Penguin/Viking Books for Young Readers, $22.99. (9780425287200). Grades 9+. Bausum explores the AIDS crisis in America from the beginning to the present day in an easy-to-follow narrative that is compelling and fast-paced. Including information about ACT Up, presidential administrations' funding of research and personal tales that include firsthand sources, this is an engaging and well-researched book on HIV and AIDS. Includes a timeline, source notes and bibliography.

Gonzales, Kathryn and Rayne, Karen, Ph.D. Trans+: Love, Sex, Romance, and Being You. 2019. 304p. American Psychological Association/Magination Press, $16.99 (9781433829833). Grades 10+. This inclusive guide for teens who are transgender, nonbinary, gender-nonconforming, or genderfluid is written by trans authors and addresses topics such as mental and physical health, reproduction, transitioning, relationships, sex, and life as a trans person. The inclusion of multiple perspectives from actual trans people, and understandable and relatable language, not to mention backmatter of links to other resources makes this a valuable resource for trans+ teens, young adults, and the people who love them.

*Hutchinson, Shaun David. Brave Face. 2019. 368p. Simon & Schuster/Simon Pulse, $18.99. (9781534431515). Grades 10+. Memoir. Author Shaun David Hutchinson explores growing up, discovering his sexual identity and facing life-threatening depression in his memoir of his teen and young adult years. Hutchinson survives a suicide attempt and embarks on a journey of recovery and self-acceptance in this honest and, at times, humorous memoir.

Young Adult Fiction
Berquist, Emma. Missing, Presumed Dead. 2019. 369p. HarperCollins/Greenwillow Books, $17.99 (9780062642813). Grades 8+. Supernatural Thriller. With a single touch, Lexi has the power to see the moment of how and when someone will die. This, combined with her ability to see ghosts, often leaves her stumbling for the comfort of a psychiatric ward for a respite. One night, Lexi literally bumps into Jane, a girl who will be murdered hours later. Jane's ghost desperately needs Lexi's help to catch the murderer before they strike again.

Boteju, Tanya. Kings, Queens, and In-Betweens. 2019. 384p. Simon & Schuster/Simon Pulse, $18.99 (9781534430655). Grades 9+. Realistic Fiction. Insecure, self-conscious Nima wants her life to be less boring. She starts with a drag show where she befriends Diedre, a trans drag queen, and Winnow, a young drag king. But can Nima pursue her new friendships without losing her old ones? And what's going on with her mom, who's suddenly gotten back in touch after walking out more than a year ago with no explanation?

Bowman, Akemi Dawn. Summer Bird Blue. 2018. 369p. Simon & Schuster/Simon Pulse, $18.99 (9781481487757). Grades 7+. Realistic Fiction. Rumi's world falls apart when her sister dies suddenly. To make things worse, her mother ships her off to live with an aunt in Hawaii. She struggles to navigate her grief and sense of abandonment with the help of her new neighbors, a teenage surfer and a taciturn 80-year-old.

Cameron, Sophie. Last Bus to Everland. 2019. 336p. Macmillan/Roaring Brook Press, $17.88 (9781250149930). Grades 9+. Fantasy. Brody feels alone in his small apartment he shares with his stressed mom, agoraphobic dad, genius older brother, and theatrical younger sister. So when his cat runs off and leads him to meet a handsome, costumed stranger, he'll take whatever escape he can get. The door to Everland only opens at 11:21 on Thursdays, but will he choose to stay or go when the doors start closing for good?

Capetta, Amy Rose. The Brilliant Death. 2018. 352p. Penguin/Viking Books for Young Readers, $18.99 (9780451478443). Grades 9+. Fantasy. Teo is a strega who has just turned one of her father's enemies into a music box when a stray cloud materializes into a person on the mountain. After her father is poisoned and the heads of the other Five Families murdered, Teo and Cielo use their strega powers to confront the person responsible in Vinalia's capital.

Capetta, Amy Rose. The Lost Coast. 2019. 352p. Candlewick, $17.99 (9781536200966). Grades 9+. Fantasy. Danny is drawn to the wild California Redwood Coast by a coven of queer teen witches called The Grays. The Grays are convinced that Danny is the only one who can save their leader, Imogen, who has disappeared–and who also may be a victim or the cause of some deadly magic that has settled there.

Clare, Cassandra and Chu, Wesley. The Red Scrolls of Magic. 2019.

368p. Simon & Schuster/Margaret K. McElderry Books, $24.99 (9781481495080). Grades 8+. Fantasy. Part of the Shadowhunter's universe and the first book in The Eldest Curses series, The Red Scrolls of Magic features High Warlock Magnus Bane and his new boyfriend, Alec Lightwood. Readers don't need to have read previous books in this universe to enjoy the wild ride as Bane, Lightwood and a cast of diverse characters tear through Europe on a quest to stop a demon-worshipping cult so they can go back to enjoying their vacation together.

Drake, Julia. The Last True Poets of the Sea. 2019. 400p. Disney/Hyperion, $17.99 (9781368048088). Grades 8+. Realistic fiction. Violet's hard-partying ways escalate the same time her brother, Sam, attempts to take his life, so her parents send her to stay with her uncle in a small Maine town where she and Sam used to spend summers. There, she immerses herself in the mission to locate the shipwreck in which her ancestor was the sole survivor. She is joined by a group of local teens, led by the enigmatic Liv. As Violet untangles the threads of her family's past, she finds herself falling for Liv.

*Emezi, Akwaeke. Pet. 2019. 203p. Random House Children's Books/Make Me A World, $17.99 (9780525647072). Grades 7+. Speculative Fiction. In Jam and Redemption's hometown of Lucille, there are no monsters anymore — or so they've always been taught. But when a creature emerges from Jam's mother's painting and claims it's here to hunt a monster, Jam and Redemption must reconsider what they thought they knew, and answer the question: how do you hunt monsters if no one will admit they even exist?

Fowley-Doyle, Moïra. All the Bad Apples. 2019. 314p. Penguin/Kathy Dawson Books, $17.99 (9780525552741). Grades 9+. Realistic Fiction. The women in the Rys family have always been labeled as "bad apples." When Deena Rys receives impossible letters from the older sister who jumped off a cliff, she and her friends set off on a journey across Ireland. Together they trace the path of the Rys women's history and the curse that's always followed them. Deena struggles to find a way to heal her family and give voice to the horrific abuse her ancestors endured.

Goslee, S. J. How (Not) to Ask a Boy to Prom. 2019. 240p. Macmillan/Roaring Brook Press, $17.99 (9781626724013). Grades 9+. Realistic fiction. Nolan is perfectly fine opting out of social engagements to stay home and draw narwhals, but his big sister has other plans. She pushes Nolan into asking his secret crush, Si O'Mara, to the prom. His prom-posal goes horribly wrong when Bern accepts the invitation instead. Nolan and Bern start fake-dating and soon lines begin to blur of what is real between them.

Grant, Mira. Alien: Echo. 2019. 304p. Macmillan/Imprint, $18.99 (9781250306296). Grades 10+. Science fiction/Horror. Olivia and her chronically ill twin sister, Viola, live on the planet Zagreus with their xenobiologist parents. When Olivia hosts a party for her sort-of girlfriend, Kora, and a few classmates, deadly xenomorphs invade the planet – which also leads to the exposure a shocking family secret. Olivia, Viola, and Kora must figure out a way to escape these terrifying aliens as well as adapt to how their lives have been completely turned upside down.

Griffin, Sarah Maria. Other Words for Smoke. 2019. 352p. Greenwillow Books, $17.99 (9780062408914). Ages 9+. Horror. Twins Mae and Rossa's lives are changed when they stay with their aunt whose house is full of secrets, mystery, and maybe even demons. This horror tale is both about a family and their secrets as well as the history of Ireland's mistreatment of women.

Hawkins, Rachel. Her Royal Highness. 2018. 274p. Penguin/G. P. Putnam's Sons, $17.99 (9781524738266). Ages 7+. Romance. When Millie Quint arrives at Gregorstoun, one of Scotland's most exclusive boarding schools, everything seems perfect – except for her roommate, Flora, who just happens to be the princess of Scotland. At first, they can't stand one another, but soon Millie finds herself falling for the princess. Millie doubts her chances of a happily-ever-after because, after all, real life isn't a fairytale.

Hutchinson, Shaun David. The Past and Other Things That Should Stay Buried. 2019. 297p. Simon & Schuster/Simon Pulse, $18.99 (9781481498579). Grades 9+. Speculative fiction. July may be dead, but that doesn't stop her from waking up in Dino's family's funeral home. Being thrown into this bizarre reality, the former best friends revisit the past as they navigate the surreal circumstances of the present.

Johnson, Lana Wood. Technically, You Started It. 2019. 374p. Scholastic/Scholastic Press, $18.99 (9781338335460). Grades 7+. Realistic Fiction. Haley's classmate randomly sends her a text, and she thinks she knows who sent it. The text is from Martin Nathaniel Munroe II – but there happen to be two students in Haley's class with this exact same name! Told entirely in text messages between Martin and Haley, this novel explores a case of mistaken identity as they build an unexpected friendship. But Haley needs to figure out which Martin is really sending the texts before their budding relationship turns into an epic disaster.

Johnston, E.K. The Afterward. 2019. 352p. Penguin/Dutton Books, $17.99 (9780735231894). Grades 9+. Fantasy. A year after the epic quest that brought Apprentice Knight Kalanthe and thief Olsa together, the two are torn apart by Kalanthe's need to find a husband who can pay off her knight school loans.

Keplinger, Kody. That's Not What Happened. 2018. 336p. Scholastic, $18.99 (9781338186529). Grades 8+. Realistic fiction. Three years after a mass school shooting, Lee and the other survivors are still trying to come to terms with what happened that day. While Lee has to decide if she should tell the truth about the details surrounding her best friend's death, she also has to deal with what comes after high school, prom, and how to explain to her friends that she is asexual.

*Khan, Sabina. The Love & Lies of Rukhsana Ali. 2019. 336p. Scholastic, $17.99 (9781338227017). Grades 9+. Realistic fiction. Rukhsana, a Bangladeshi-American teenager, must balance her life between conservative Muslim parents and her friends who don't understand her family and culture. Rukhsana knows her family will not approve of her love life – she's secretly dating a girl. Her parents discover the relationship and send her to relatives in Bangladesh to marry a nice, young Bengali man. Rukhsana finds unlikely allies as she carves out her own path to live the way she chooses.

Kisner, Adrienne. The Confusion of Laurel Graham. 2019. 288p.

Macmillan/Feiwel & Friends, $17.99 (9781250146045). Grades 9+. Realistic fiction. Laurel wants to become a famous birder and nature photographer. When her grandmother is hospitalized after an accident while tracking a mysterious bird call, Laurel knows she must find and document this bird. Not only will she finish what her grandmother started, but Laurel is certain it will ensure her a winning entry into the junior nature photographer contest. But standing in her way is the girl she suspects sabotaged her earlier photos – and Laurel just might be falling for her.

*Konigsberg, Bill. The Music of What Happens. 2019. 342p. Scholastic/Arthur A. Levine Books, $17.99 (9781338215502). Ages 9+. Realistic fiction. A chance encounter leads Max to help Jordan run a quirky food truck, which may be the only thing standing between Jordan and his severely depressed mother from becoming homeless. Max is hiding his own trauma, while Jordan is struggling with the responsibility of taking care of his mother and the resentment his feels towards his two best friends. Opposites attract as they struggle to face their demons.

Lawson, Rich. Annex. 2018. 368p. Hachette/Orbit, $15.99 (9780316416542). Grades 8+.Science fiction. Aliens have invaded Earth, turning adult humans into mindless drones and young people into hosts for their Parasites. A small group of kids, led by the charismatic Wyatt, have escaped the aliens and scrape by on their own. Violet, a white trans girl, and Bo, a Nigerien-American boy, discover Wyatt isn't the savior that he seems to be, but they'll have to work with him anyway if they're going to save the world.

Legrand, Claire. Sawkill Girls. 2019. 464p. HarperCollins/Katherine Tegen Books, $17.99 (9780062696601). Grades 9+. Horror. People have been disappearing for decades on the island of Sawkill Rock, but lately those disappearances have been getting more frequent. As the horror comes closer and closer, Val, Marion, and Zoey must work together to find a way to thwart the evil that preys on their home.

London, Alex. Black Wings Beating. 2018. 432p. Macmillan/Farrar, Straus and Giroux Books for Young Readers, $17.99 (9780374306823). Grades 8+. Fantasy. In a world that revolves around birding and falconry, fraternal twins Brysen and Kylee are often at odds. He's determined to be a great falconer but lacks skill, while Kylee is gifted but antagonistic towards the craft. Still, the siblings rely on each other to survive. When Brysen has to capture the elusive and lethal Ghost Eagle in order to save his boyfriend's life, Kylee accompanies him, despite her own misgivings.

McCarthy, Cori and Capetta, Amy Rose. Once & Future. 2019. 368p. Hachette/Little, Brown/Jimmy Patterson, $18.99 (9780316449274). Grades 9+. Science Fiction/Fantasy. In this sci-fi reimagining of Arthurian legend, Ari Helix draws together a band of fighters, including a now-teenaged Merlin, and her friends to fight a tyrannical, intergalactic corporation that has been exploiting the residents of some planets and destroying others. To make matters worse, Morgana, Merlin's nemesis, is determined to free the soul of the original Arthur, locked inside of Ari.

McLemore, Anna-Marie. Blanca & Roja. 2018. 384p. Macmillan/Feiwel and Friends, $17.99 (9781250162717). Grades 8+. Magical Realism/Fairy Tale Adaptation. For generations, there have always been two daughters in the del Cisne family, and destiny dictates that shortly after the younger sister's 15th birthday, one sister will turn into a swan and the other will remain human. When two local missing children reappear in the woods near the sisters' home, Blanca and Roja's bond is tested. They find themselves confronting their ideas about family, love, and identity while waiting expectantly to discover their fate.

*Mejia, Tehlor Kay. We Set the Dark on Fire. 2019. 364p. HarperCollins/Katherine Tegen Books, $17.99 (9780062691316). Grades 9+. Speculative Fiction. Daniela Vargas is the Medio School for Girls' top student, and upon her graduation, she's guaranteed a life of comfort and luxury as she's picked to be one of two wives to the city's most promising young bachelor. As Primera, she's been through years of rigid training, but nothing prepares her for the decisions she'll have to make after her marriage — especially not when she's asked to spy for the resistance, or when she finds herself falling for someone forbidden.

Mitchell, Saundra. All the Things We Do in the Dark. 2019. 304p. HarperCollins/HarperTeen, $17.99 (9780062852595). Grades 8+.

Thriller. Something happened when Ava was nine; the scar on her face is proof of that much. After spending years trying to build a life and stuff trauma down, she trips over a dead body in the woods while walking back from getting a tattoo. Is this death and her trauma connected in any way other than in Ava's mind? And what about Haley, the cute girl Ava's falling for, who just happens to be the daughter of the first in a string of police office she talked to all those years ago? Contains resources for sexual abuse and assault survivors.

Mitchell, Saundra. The Prom: A Novel Based on the Hit Broadway Musical. 2019. 240p. Penguin/Viking Books for Young Readers, $17.99 (9781984837523). Grades 8+. Realistic Fiction/Romance. The only thing Emma wants is to dance with her girlfriend Alyssa at prom, but the PTA in her small town is determined not to let them "ruin" prom for the rest of the students. Enter two slightly washed-up Broadway stars with their own agenda, pushing Emma and Alyssa to fight for what they want.

Montgomery, Candace. By Any Means Necessary. 2019. 320p. Page Street Publishing Co., $17.99 (9781624147999). Grades 10+. Realistic Fiction. Torrence "Torrey" McKenzie is ready to make a fresh start as a freshman in college. But no sooner does he leave then he finds out that the family apiary is about to be seized by the city and there's not enough money to pay the back taxes to save it. Torrey struggles with the decision to go back and save the apiary from developers or stay in school and make a new life for himself.

Muir, Tamsyn. Gideon the Ninth. 2019. 444p. Tor/Tom Doherty Associates/Macmillan Publishing Group, LLC, $25.99 (9781250313195). Grades 10+. Science Fiction. When the Emperor summons the heirs of each of the solar system's Houses to a necromantic trial of wits and skill, Harrowhark Nonagesimus forces Gideon to accompany her as her cavalier. If Harrowhark succeeds, she'll become immortal — but without Gideon's sword, she'll fail, and the Ninth House will die with her. Then dead bodies start turning up. Can Gideon and Harrow stay alive long enough to solve the Emperor's puzzle?

Nazemian, Abdi. Like a Love Story. 2019. 432p. HarperCollins/Balzer + Bray, $17.99 (9780062839367). Grades 10+.

Historical Fiction. Set in 1989 NYC against the backdrop of the AIDS crisis, the story of three teens intertwine: Reza, a recent Iranian immigrant battling his attraction to other men; Art, an out-and-proud activist and photographer; and Judy, a plus-size fashion designer and Art's best friend, whose uncle is dying of AIDS. In an attempt to avoid the truth about himself, Reza starts dating Judy. Soon she falls in love with him, but he's fallen in love with Art. Can Reza untangle this web without losing his friends?

Petras, Junaunda. The Stars and the Blackness Between Them. 2019. 320p. Penguin/Dutton Books for Young Readers, $17.99 (9780525555483). Grades 9+. Realistic fiction. When Audre's mother catches her with the pastor's daughter, she's shipped off from her home in Trinidad to live with her father in Minneapolis. There, she meets and falls for Mabel, who is questioning not only her own romantic feelings, but also why she's been feeling ill all summer.

Philips, L. Sometime After Midnight. 2018. 385p. Penguin/Viking Books for Young Readers, $18.99 (9780425291634). Grades 10+.Romance/Fairy Tale Adaptation. Aspiring musicians Cameron and Nate meet and immediately click, but Nate runs away when he learns that Cameron is heir to the record-label that destroyed his dad's life. The only evidence of their meeting is the photo of Nate's sharpie-covered Chuck Taylors, which Cam's sister posts online to help Prince Charming track down his Cinderfella.

Poston, Ashley. The Princess and the Fangirl. 2019. 316p. Quirk Books, $18.99 (9781683690962). Grades 10+. Fairy Tale Adaptation. While Imogen wants to save a character in a movie franchise, the actress who plays the character, Jessica, would like to leave. When they meet at a fan convention, they are mistaken for each other. After the super-secret script to the Starfield sequel leaks, suddenly all fingers are pointed at Jessica. Jessica and Imogen agree to switch places to discover the culprit.

Roehrig, Caleb. Death Prefers Blondes. 2019. 448 p. Macmillan/Feiwel & Friends, 17.99 (9781250155825). Grades 10+. Thriller/Suspense. Wealthy socialite Margo Manning and her found family of struggling but exuberant young men pull off elaborate heists while in their drag queen personas. When Margo's father's death spurs her to take on a risky job, her friends must decide how far they are willing to stick by her side in this fun, sexy thriller.

Rowell, Rainbow. Wayward Son. 2019. 356p. Macmillan/St. Martin's/Wednesday Books, $19.99 (9781250146076). Grades 9+. Fantasy/Paranormal Romance. Simon, Penny, and Baz triumphed over the villain in Carry On, but the happy ending hasn't turned out like they expected. Without his powers, Simon is a couch potato with wings, and the hope of a real relationship between Simon and Baz has gone nowhere. When an opportunity arises to ride to the rescue, the three embark on a road trip across the American West.

Russo, Meredith. Birthday. 2019. 278p. Macmillan/St. Martin's/Flatiron, $18.99 (9781250129833). Grades 9+. Realistic Fiction. Eric and Morgan's families were thrust together the day they were born when they were all snowed-in at the hospital thanks to a freak, out-of-season September blizzard that hit their Tennessee community. Over the course of six birthdays, their lives unfold in complex and beautiful ways.

Ryan, Tom. Keep This to Yourself. 2019. 309p. Albert Whitman, $17.99 (9780807541517). Grades 9+. Mystery/Thriller. A year ago, Mac's best friend Connor was the final victim of a serial killer who tore through their tiny town. As the school year ends, Mac finds a note from Connor asking to meet – a note left in a comic book from the night he died. Mac teams up with friends to solve the mystery of who killed four people, and why the murders suddenly stopped after Connor's death.

Schrieve, Hal. Out of Salem. 2019. 448p. Seven Stories Press, $19.95 (9781609809010). Grades 8+. Paranormal Fiction. Z is nonbinary and recently lost their family in the car crash that turned Z into a zombie. Now, Z is under suspicion from their uncle, their classmates, and society in general. They're soon befriended by Aysel, a werewolf of Turkish descent, and Tommy, a boy who's bullied for his alleged fey ancestry. When werewolves are blamed for the death of a local man, anti-monster sentiment rises, including in local law enforcement, which puts all three teens at risk.

Shrum, Brianna R. Kissing Ezra Holtz (and Other Things I Did for

Science). 2019. 277p. Sky Horse/Sky Pony Press, $16.99 (9781510749405). Grades 9+. Realistic Fiction/Romance. Of course Amalia's AP Psychology teacher pairs her up for a group project with the guy from her synagogue she's been avoiding her whole life. For their project, she and Ezra decide to bring back a study that suggests it can make any two people fall in love. As they refine their experiment on others, it might actually be working on them.

Silverman, Laura. You Asked for Perfect. 2019. 267p. Sourcebooks/Sourcebooks Fire, $10.99 (9781492658276). Grades 9+. Realistic Fiction. Ariel is stressed out trying to make sure everything about his high school years is perfect so that he can get into the best college. But after failing a calculus quiz, he asks Amir to tutor him. Math may not be Ariel's thing, but Amir might just be perfect for him.

Smedley, Zack. Deposing Nathan. 2019. 393p. Page Street Publishing Co., $17.99 (9781624147357). Grades 10+. Realistic Fiction. Nate is a devout Catholic who lives under the thumb of his overly strict aunt and never breaks the rules, until he meets Cam, who is whip-smart, irreverent, and rebellious. Despite their differences, the two quickly become friends and then, maybe, something more. But when Cam comes out as bi and expects Nate to do the same, he's met instead with violent biphobia and homophobia. Through flashbacks and deposition testimony, Nate tells the story of how Cam met him, quickly became his closest friend, and ended up stabbing him in the stomach.

Solomon, Rachel Lynn. Our Year of Maybe. 384p. Simon & Schuster/Simon Pulse, $18.99 (9781481497763). Grades 9+. Realistic Fiction. Sophie and Peter have been best friends forever, even after Sophie turned down Peter's romantic advance in middle school. Now they're in high school and Sophie's the one in love with him, but after she donates a kidney to Peter, they find themselves growing further apart rather than closer. Will Peter's reinvigorated life mean the death of their friendship?

Sterling, Isabel. These Witches Don't Burn. 2019. 320p. Penguin Books/Razorbill, $17.99 (9780451480323). Grades 8+. Fantasy/Supernatural Romance. Hannah and her family are descended from a line of Elemental Witches. Her life consists of avoiding her ex and selling souvenirs to Salem tourists. When a blood ritual interrupts the end-of-school bonfire, Hannah is convinced it's the work of a Blood Witch. While trying to smoke out the culprit, Hannah meets Morgan, a cute girl who's new to town. But she learns it's so hard to date when trying to stop a string of deadly attacks.

Thomas, Leah. Wild and Crooked. 2019. 438p. Bloomsbury/Bloomsbury YA, $18.99 (9781547600021). Grades 9+. Realistic Fiction. Whether because of her infamous family history, their low-class status, or her sexuality, Kaylyn is used to others picking on her. When she attends a new high school, she uses a fake name to avoid notoriety and pretends to be a nice Southern Belle. She is surprised to find herself among the popular students. But she also befriends one of the least popular – Gus Peake who's known as "the disabled kid" because of his cerebral palsy. When Kaylyn's family history comes to light, their small town explodes in anger.

Vale, Lillie. Small Town Hearts. 2019. 324p. Macmillan/Swoon Reads, $17.99 (9781250192356). Grades 9+. Realistic fiction/Romance. It's the summer after high school, and Babe's job as a barista in a beach town keeps her busy after breaking up with her best friends, when cute tourist Levi walks through her door. She never falls for summer boys, but he might be just what she needs to distract her from memories and the reappearance of her ex-girlfriend.

Villasante, Alexandra. The Grief Keeper. 2019. 320p. Penguin/G.P. Putnam's Sons Books for Young Readers, $17.99 (9780525514022). Grades 9+. Science Fiction/Romance. Marisol flees El Salvador with her younger sister Gabi, but they get caught crossing into the United States. When she's told her asylum request has been denied, her only hope of staying and keeping her sister safe comes from a pilot program of a new technology that funnels the grief, trauma, and pain of wealthy patrons to poor immigrants with no other choices. Her new life is nothing like the American TV shows Marisol loves so much, but in living so closely with Rey, who lost her brother during a concert, it may not only be her grief Marisol feels.

Wells, Rebecca Kim. Shatter the Sky. 2019. 294p. Simon & Schuster, $18.99 (9781534437906). Grades 9+. Fantasy. When Kaia is abducted by the empire, Maren sets off on a quest to steal a dragon, rescue her girlfriend, and save her way of life.

Wexler, Django. Ship of Smoke and Steel. 2019. Tor Teen/Macmillan Publishing Group, $17.99 (9780765397249). Grades 9+. Fantasy. Eighteen-year-old Isoka is a ward boss in a port city, using her combat magical skills to survive on the streets and providing for her sister's more comfortable existence. Captured and threatened with the life of her sister, she agrees to use her skills to attempt to steal a legendary ghost ship. To accomplish her mission, Isoka will become a part of the brutal crew, battling creatures while navigating her unexpected feelings for a fellow fighter as well as a princess with her own dark power.

Winters, Julian. How to Be Remy Cameron. 2019. Interlude/Duet, $17.99 (9781945053801). Grades 9+. Realistic Fiction. Remy Cameron is black, adopted, and gay… but who is he? When he's assigned to answer that question in a school essay, Remy is stymied. How can he know who he is when he doesn't know where he came from? And why should he be expected to have an answer at age 17, anyway? Fortunately, a birth relative connects with him on Facebook who may offer some answers. As the mystery of his identity unfurls, Remy is also working to move past a bad relationship and open up to a cute new boy in town named Ian.

Zappia, Francesca. Now Entering Addamsville. 2019. 357p. HarperCollins/Greenwillow Books, $17.99 (9780062935274). Grades 9+. Supernatural Mystery. Addamsville is no stranger to ghosts, and unlike most people who live there, Zora knows they're real because she can see them. Supernatural forces in Addamsville start causing fires that get people killed, and Zora is framed for their crimes. She'll need to track down the true culprit. In a small town obsessed with ghosts but unaware of the actual existence of spectres among them, will anyone believe the truth?

Graphic Non-Fiction
Kobabe, Maia. Gender Queer: A Memoir. 2019. 239p. Oni/Lion Forge, $17.99 (9781549304002). Grades 10+. Maia's memoir documents their life and journey of self-discovery, from cringey crushes to gay fanfic and coming out as both nonbinary and asexual.

Gillman, Melanie. Stage Dreams. 2019. 104p. Lerner/Graphic Universe, $29.32 (9781512440003). Grades 6-9. Historical Fiction. In New Mexico Territory, a Latina bandit known as the "Ghost Hawk" holds up a stagecoach and takes hostage a trans woman, Grace, who offers to help her sneak into a party where several Confederate railroad barons will be meeting. As they prepare to infiltrate high society, the women start to develop feelings for each other, and the stakes couldn't be higher.

Graley, Sarah. Kim Reaper, Volume 2: Vampire Island. 2019. 99p. Oni Press, $14.99 (9781620106372). Grade 9+. Paranormal Fantasy. Kim works overtime for her grumpy grim reaper boss and doesn't have enough time to spend with her girlfriend, Becka. She ends up going on a group date to Vampire Island with her girlfriend and Becka's roommate who Kim despises. Things quickly get out of hand when the vampires realize there are humans at the party.

O'Neill, Katie. The Tea Dragon Festival. 2019. 134p. Oni Press, Inc., $21.99 (9781620106556). Grades 4-8. Fantasy. In this prequel to The Tea Dragon Society, Rinn stumbles across a real dragon! Aedhan was assigned to guard Rinn's village but fell asleep in the forest eighty years ago. Rinn investigates the mystery of Aedhan's enchanted sleep, as well as helping Aedhan come to terms with feeling that he cannot get back the time he lost.

Pascat, C.S. Fence, Volume 1. 2018. 112p. BOOM! Box, $9.99 (9781684151929). Grades 7+. Sports Fiction. Nicholas must prove his worth as an illegitimate son of a fencing champion, so he gains acceptance at a prestigious boarding school whose fencing team has a reputation for excellence, but before he can make a name for himself, he must find a way to make it onto the fencing team and compete against the heavy favorite, Seiji – who is also his half-brother.

Pascat, C.S. Fence, Volume 2. 2019. 112p. BOOM! Box, $14.99 (9781684152971).

Pascat, C.S. Fence, Volume 3. 2019. 112p. BOOM! Box, $14.99 (9781684153343).

Steele, Hammish. DeadEndia: The Broken Halo: Book 2. 2019. 237p. Nobrow Press, $16.95 (9781910620625). Grades 9+. Paranormal Fantasy. Dead End is a hotel in a theme park, as well as a portal to hell. Norma is dealing with unwanted ghosts while trying to keep the hotel running, Barney is secretly (and literally) wrestling demons, and neither of them are sure if they are even still friends. All the while, a war is brewing across the thirteen planes and Dead End is somehow right in the center of everything.

Sturges, Lilah. Lumberjanes: The Infernal Compass. 2018. 144p. BOOM! Box, $14.99 (9781684152520). Grades 9+. Fantasy. In this prequel to the Lumberjanes graphic novel series, the Janes set out to earn their orienteering badge—only their compass seems to possess some mystical qualities. At the same time, Molly and Mal are each orienting themselves in their new relationship, while concerned about its effect on their group of friends.

Tamaki, Mariko. Laura Dean Keeps Breaking Up with Me. 2019. 304p. Macmillan/Holtzbrinck/Roaring Brook Press/First Second,

$17.99 (9781626722590). Grades 8+. Realistic Fiction. Freddy is addicted to her popular, attractive girlfriend—the titular Laura Dean—even though Laura has broken up with her twice. Laura disrespects Freddy's time, friends, and heart. Things come to a head when Freddy's best friend is in crisis on the same day as Laura's birthday party.

Templer, Hannah. Cosmoknights. 2019. 211p. Idea and Design Works/IDW Publishing/Top Shelf Productions, $19.99 (9781603094542). Grades 10+. Science Fiction. When a charismatic pair of off-world gladiators show up on Pan's doorstep, she just wants to get them patched up and on their way. But their talk intrigues her, and soon she follows them off the galactic grid, learning the secrets of her world — and discovering the chance to burn it all down.

Usdin, Carly. The Avant-Guards, Volume 1. 2019. 112p. BOOM! Box, $14.99 (9781684153671). Grades 9+. Sports Fiction. Charlie transfers to art school in the hopes of getting a new start. When the spirited Olivia tries to recruit her to the school's (admittedly terrible)

basketball team, Charlie is hesitant—she used to be a basketball star but left it all behind. When she does finally decide to join the team, she and the other players find themselves learning to trust and support one another.

Walden, Tillie. On a Sunbeam. 2018. 535p. Macmillan/Holtzbrinck/Roaring Brook Press/First Second, $21.99 (9781250178138). Grades 8+. Science fiction. A romantic space adventure that spans the halls of the boarding school where Mia and Grace fell in love, to the ancient structures on distant planets in the far reaches of the galaxy. Separated under mysterious circumstances, Mia is determined to reunite with Grace – and she will brave anything to find her again.

https://glbtrt.ala.org/rainbowbooks/about

End

Let there be light, Lord.

10 – INDOCTRINATION THROUGH ENTERTAINMENT

Hollywood has indeed come out of the closet in our theaters and television in recent years and the GLAAD Organization had much to do with it. Here is their story in their own words for readers to consider.

GLAAD

From Wikipedia, the free encyclopedia [1]

Not to be confused with GLBTQ Legal Advocates & Defenders.

GLAAD is an American non-governmental media monitoring organization founded by LGBT people in the media. Before March 2013, the name "GLAAD" had been an acronym for "Gay & Lesbian Alliance Against Defamation" but became the primary name due to its inclusiveness of bisexual and transgender issues.

History

Formed in New York City in 1985 to protest against what it saw as the New York Post's defamatory and sensationalized AIDS coverage, GLAAD put pressure on media organizations to end what it saw as homophobic reporting. Initial meetings were held in the homes of several New York City activists as well as after-hours at the New York State Council on the Arts. The founding group included film scholar Vito Russo; Gregory Kolovakos, then on the staff of the NYS Arts Council and who later became the first executive director; Darryl Yates Rist; Allen Barnett; Jewelle Gomez, the organization's first treasurer; and film critic Marcia Pally, who later served as acting Board chair. Some members of GLAAD went on to become the early members of ACT UP.

103

In 1987, after a meeting with GLAAD, The New York Times changed its editorial policy to use the word "gay" instead of harsher terms referring to homosexuality. GLAAD advocated that the Associated Press and other television and print news sources follow. GLAAD's influence soon spread to Los Angeles, where organizers began working with the entertainment industry to change the way LGBT people were portrayed on screen.

Entertainment Weekly has named GLAAD as one of Hollywood's most powerful entities, and the Los Angeles Times described GLAAD as "possibly one of the most successful organizations lobbying the media for inclusion".

Within the first five years of its founding in New York as the Gay and Lesbian Anti-Defamation League (soon after changed to "Gay & Lesbian Alliance Against Defamation" after legal pressure by the Anti-Defamation League), GLAAD chapters had been established in Los Angeles and other cities, with the LA chapter becoming particularly influential due to its proximity to the California entertainment industry. GLAAD/NY and GLAAD/LA would eventually vote to merge in 1994, with other city chapters joining soon afterward; however, the chapters continue to exist, with the ceremonies of the GLAAD Media Awards being divided each year into three ceremonies held in New York City, Los Angeles and San Francisco.

Following the 2011 resignation of Jarrett Barrios from the GLAAD presidency, Mike Thompson served as interim president until the announcement of Herndon Graddick, previously GLAAD's Vice-President of Programs and Communications, to the presidency on April 15, 2012. Graddick is the younger son of Charles Graddick of Mobile, a circuit court judge and the former Attorney General of Alabama.

In 2013, Jennifer Finney Boylan was chosen as the first openly transgender co-chair of GLAAD's National Board of Directors.[8]

Programs

GLAAD Media Awards

The GLAAD Media Awards were established in 1989. Ceremonies are held annually in New York City, Los Angeles and San Francisco.

Announcing Equality Project

Established in 2002, GLAAD's Announcing Equality project has resulted in more than 1,000 newspapers including gay and lesbian announcements alongside other wedding listings.

Commentator Accountability Project

In March 2012, GLAAD launched the Commentator Accountability Project, which seeks to index and document frequent contributors, guests and pundits who regularly express anti-LGBT bias and misinformation in their contributions to journalistic outlets.

Studio Responsibility Index

In August 2013, GLAAD launched its first annual Studio Responsibility Index, which indexes "the quantity, quality and diversity of images of LGBT people in films released by six major motion picture studios".

GLAAD Media Reference Guide

The GLAAD Media Reference Guide is a style guide of recommendations for writers, especially journalistic outlets, to reference in positive, inclusive depiction of LGBT people. It has been published since the 1990s (then known as the GLAAD Media Guide to the Lesbian and Gay Community), with the 10th edition, being the most recent, published in 2016.

Movements

GLAAD has begun the Together Movement, which encourages all to join in support of those discriminated against including women, Muslims, immigrants and members of the LGBTQ+ community.

In 2010, GLAAD launched Spirit Day. Spirit Day is an annual national day of action to show LGBTQ youth that they are not alone because there is plenty of support all around them.[17]

In 2016, Spirit Day is the world's largest and most-visible anti-bullying campaign.

The campaign works to bring anti-bullying resources to classrooms all around the world by inspiring educators to take action against bullying through hosting events and rallies. The campaign also created a GLAAD's Spirit Day kit for use in classrooms, which is available in 6 languages.

On social media, people are encouraged to wear purple or go purple online in order to stand united against bullying. Huge media companies such as NBC Universal and Viacom show support for Spirit Day on the airwaves. They even change their on-air logo to purple for the day. They also enlist talent who wear purple during the day's broadcast.[17]

More than 1.5 billion media impressions annually are seen in support of the campaign. The hashtag #Spirit Day has become a trending topic on Twitter and Facebook every year. On social media, people such as Oprah Winfrey, Ellen DeGeneres and President Barack Obama have shown their support for the campaign.[17]

Media

Over the past two decades, Americans have experienced a significant evolution in their understanding and cultural acceptance of lesbian, gay, bisexual, transgender, and queer (LGBTQ) people.

Consequently, media coverage of LGBTQ issues has moved beyond simplistic political dichotomies and toward more fully realized representations, not only of the diversity of the LGBTQ community, but also of LGBTQ people's lives, their families, and their fundamental inclusion in the fabric of American society. Today, LGBTQ people's stories are more likely to be told in the same way as others — with fairness, integrity, and respect. Journalists realize that LGBTQ people have the right to fair, accurate, and inclusive reporting of their stories and their issues, and GLAAD's Media Reference Guide, now in its tenth edition, offers tools they can use to tell LGBTQ people's stories in ways that bring out the best in journalism.

GLAAD's Media Reference Guide is intended to be used by

journalists reporting for mainstream media outlets and by creators in entertainment media who want to tell LGBTQ people's stories fairly and accurately. It is not intended to be an all-inclusive glossary of language used within the LGBTQ community, nor is it a prescriptive guide for LGBTQ people.Media

Over the past two decades, Americans have experienced a significant evolution in their understanding and cultural acceptance of lesbian, gay, bisexual, transgender, and queer (LGBTQ) people.

Consequently, media coverage of LGBTQ issues has moved beyond simplistic political dichotomies and toward more fully realized representations, not only of the diversity of the LGBTQ community, but also of LGBTQ people's lives, their families, and their fundamental inclusion in the fabric of American society. Today, LGBTQ people's stories are more likely to be told in the same way as others — with fairness, integrity, and respect. Journalists realize that LGBTQ people have the right to fair, accurate, and inclusive reporting of their stories and their issues, and GLAAD's Media Reference Guide, now in its tenth edition, offers tools they can use to tell LGBTQ people's stories in ways that bring out the best in journalism.

GLAAD's Media Reference Guide is intended to be used by journalists reporting for mainstream media outlets and by creators in entertainment media who want to tell LGBTQ people's stories fairly and accurately. It is not intended to be an all-inclusive glossary of language used within the LGBTQ community, nor is it a prescriptive guide for LGBTQ people.

References:

[1]"Barnett, Allen (1955–1991)". glbtq.com. Archived from the original on October 15, 2012. Retrieved March 25, 2013.

[2]Politics of Ego: GLAAD Saga Unravelled, in Gay Community News, p.3 (March 1-7, 1987)

[3 "GLAAD for Clay Aiken". Claynewsnetwork.com. Archived from the original on 2013-05-28. Retrieved 2013-12-03.

[4] Anderson, Tre'vell (2016-05-02). "Here is why Hollywood also

has an LGBT diversity issue". Los Angeles Times. Retrieved 2020-06-13.

[6] "Entertainment Weekly's 101 Most Influential People (1992)". Amiannoying.com. 1976-11-25. Archived from the original on 2012-04-19. Retrieved 2013-12-03.

[7] Myers and Cress 2004: 200

[8] Reynolds, Daniel (2013-11-08). "GLAAD Appoints First Transgender Cochair". Advocate.com. Archived from the original on 2013-11-11. Retrieved 2013-12-03.

[9] Peeples, Jase (March 24, 2013). "GLAAD Affirms Commitment To Trans and Bi People, Alters Name". The Advocate. Archived from the original on March 27, 2013. Retrieved March 25, 2013.

[10] The woman who saved GLAAD: how Sarah Kate Ellis brought the faltering nonprofit into the 21st century. Author: Setoodeh Journal: Variety ISSN: 0042-2738 Date: 09/27/2016 Volume: 333 Issue: 12 Page: 50

[11]Reynolds, Daniel (November 25, 2013). "GLAAD Announces Sarah Kate Ellis as President". The Advocate. Archived from the original on December 2, 2013. Retrieved January 18, 2014.[12]"Announcing Equality". glaad.org. Archived from the original on September 1, 2011. Retrieved March 25, 2013.

[12] "Commentator Accountability Project (CAP)". GLAAD. Archived from the original on 2013-01-16. Retrieved 2013-02-16.

[13]' Max Gouttebroze (August 21, 2013). "First annual Studio Responsibility Index finds lack of substantial LGBT characters in mainstream films". GLAAD. Archived from the original on September 29, 2013. Retrieved October 7, 2013.

[14] ""GLAAD Publications", as archived on 5 February 1997". Web.archive.org. 1997-02-05. Archived from the original on 1997-02-05. Retrieved 2013-12-03.

[15] "Media Reference Guide – 9th Edition". GLAAD. Archived from the original on 2015-07-29. Retrieved 2015-08-04.

[17]"Take the Together Pledge". GLAAD. 2017-01-31. Archived from the original on 2017-09-29. Retrieved 2017-09-29.

[18]GLAAD hopes to stem bullying of LGBTQ youth on Spirit Day Author: Adams, S. Journal: PRweek (U.S. ed.) ISSN: 1524-1696 Date: 08/01/2016 Volume: 19 Issue: 8 Page: 16

https://en.wikipedia.org/wiki/GLAAD

End

11 – CONQUERING THE COURTS

The U.S. Supreme Court, on June 26, 2015, ruled that the U.S. Constitution provides same-sex couples the right to marry thereby handing a historic triumph to the American gay rights movement. But legalizing gay marriage was an easy decision for our politically correct Supreme Court in light of the number of gay organizations that demonstrated, marched, and camped outside their magnificent structure in Washington D.C. The justices must have reasoned that if the American Psychological Association changed its mind on their definition of homosexuality, churches changed their mind on the morals of same sex marriage, and schools changed their mind on educating children about homosexual acts, then the Court could change our laws to identify gays as a protected class of person.

Landmark U.S. Supreme Court Ruling Legalizes Gay Marriage Nationwide

U.S. NEWS

By Lawrence Hurley

JUNE 27, 201510:18 PM UPDATED 6 YEARS AGO

WASHINGTON (Reuters) - The Supreme Court ruled on Friday that the U.S. Constitution provides same-sex couples the right to marry, handing a historic triumph to the American gay rights movement.

The court ruled 5-4 that the Constitution's guarantees of due process and equal protection under the law mean that states cannot ban same-sex marriages. With the landmark ruling, gay marriage becomes legal in all 50 states.

Immediately after the decision, same-sex couples in many of states where gay marriage had been banned headed to county clerks' offices for marriage licenses as state officials issued statements saying they would respect the ruling.

President Barack Obama, appearing in the White House Rose Garden, hailed the ruling as a milestone in American justice that arrived "like a thunderbolt."

"This ruling is a victory for America," said Obama, the first sitting president to support gay marriage. "This decision affirms what millions of Americans already believe in their hearts. When all Americans are treated as equal, we are all more free."

Justice Anthony Kennedy, writing on behalf of the court, said the hope of gay people intending to marry

"is not to be condemned to live in loneliness, excluded from one of civilization's oldest institutions. They ask for equal dignity in the eyes of the law. The Constitution grants them that right."

Kennedy, a conservative who often casts the deciding vote in close cases, was joined in the majority by the court's four liberal justices.

Kennedy, appointed by Republican President Ronald Reagan in 1988, has now authored all four of the court's major gay rights rulings, with the first coming in 1996. As with his 2013 opinion when the court struck down a federal law that denied benefits to same-sex couples, Kennedy stressed the dignity of marriage.

"Without the recognition, stability and predictability marriage offers, their children suffer the stigma of knowing their families are somehow lesser," Kennedy wrote.

In a blistering dissenting opinion, conservative Justice Antonin Scalia said the decision shows the court is a

"threat to American democracy." The ruling "says that my ruler and the ruler of 320 million Americans coast-to-coast is a majority of the nine lawyers on the Supreme Court," Scalia added.

Conservative Chief Justice John Roberts read a summary of his dissent from the bench, the first time he has done so in his 10 years on the court. Roberts said although there are strong policy arguments in same-sex marriage, it was not the court's role to force states to change their marriage laws.

"Five lawyers have closed the debate and enacted their own vision of marriage as a matter of constitutional law," Roberts wrote.

The dissenters raised concerns about the impact of the case on people opposed to same-sex marriage on religious grounds.

Although the ruling only affects state laws and religious institutions can still choose whether to marry same-sex couples, Roberts predicted future legal conflicts.

"Hard questions arise when people of faith exercise religion in ways that may be seen to conflict with the new right to same-sex marriage," Roberts said.

Roberts gave as an example a religious college that provides married student housing only to opposite-sex couples.

The ruling is the Supreme Court's most important expansion of marriage rights in the United States since its landmark 1967 ruling in the case Loving v. Virginia that struck down state laws barring interracial marriages.

There were 13 state bans in place, while another state, Alabama, had contested a court ruling that lifted the ban there.

The ruling is the latest milestone in the gay rights movement in recent years. In 2010, Obama signed a law allowing gays to serve openly in the U.S. military. In 2013, the high court ruled unconstitutional a 1996 U.S. law that declared for the purposes of federal benefits marriage was defined as between one man and one woman.

Reaction came swiftly. James Obergefell, the lead plaintiff in the case, told a cheering crowd outside the Supreme Court,

"Today's ruling from the Supreme Court affirms what millions across this country already know to be true in our hearts - our love is equal, that the four words etched onto the front of the Supreme Court - equal justice under law - apply to us, too."

Hundreds of gay rights supporters celebrated outside the courthouse with whoops and cries of "U-S-A!" and "Love is love" as the decision came down.

Conservatives denounced the ruling. Republican presidential candidate Mike Huckabee said, *"This flawed, failed decision is an out-of-control act of unconstitutional judicial tyranny."* Republican presidential candidate Rick Santorum lamented that five *"unelected judges redefined the foundational unit of society."*

Opponents say same-sex marriage legality should be decided by states, not judges. Some opponents argue it is an affront to traditional marriage between a man and a woman and that the Bible condemns homosexuality.

Hillary Clinton, the front-runner for the 2016 Democratic presidential nomination, wrote on Twitter she was *"proud to celebrate a historic victory for marriage equality."*

The decision follows rapid changes in attitudes and policies toward gay marriage in America. It was not until 2003 that the Supreme Court threw out state laws banning gay sex. And it was not until 2004 that the Massachusetts became the first state to legalize same-sex marriage. Gay marriage has gained increasing acceptance in opinion polls in recent years, particularly among younger Americans.

Gay marriage also is gaining acceptance in other Western countries. Last month in Ireland, voters backed same-sex marriage by a landslide in a referendum that marked a dramatic social shift in the traditionally Roman Catholic country.

Ireland followed several Western European countries including Britain, France and Spain in allowing gay marriage, which is also legal in South Africa, Brazil and Canada. But homosexuality remains taboo and often illegal in many parts of Africa and Asia.

The Supreme Court's ruling came in a consolidated case pulling together challenges filed by same-sex couples to gay marriage bans in Kentucky, Michigan, Ohio and Tennessee.

The Obama administration argued on the side of the same-sex marriage advocates.

Additional reporting by Joan Biskupic, Megan Cassella, Bill Trott, Fiona Ortiz, Mary Wisniewski, Ben Klayman, Ayesha Rascoe, Jon Herskovitz, Lindsay Dunsmuir, Any Sullivan and Roberta Rampton; Editing by Will Dunham and Leslie Adler

https://www.reuters.com/article/us-usa-court-gaymarriage-idUSKBN0P61SW20150628

End

Churches that Refuse to Perform Gay 'Marriages' May Lose Insurance Coverage

'Churches, you're on your own.'

Life Site News

By Lisa Bourne

WASHINGTON, D.C., July 10, 2015 (Life Site News) – Churches that refuse to perform homosexual "weddings" may be at risk for devastating financial losses in the wake of Obergefell v. Hodges, because insurance companies refuse to cover them.

While the Supreme Court majority gave a nod to religious liberty in its June 26 ruling decreeing homosexual "marriage" a constitutional "right," countless American churches and pastors may be exposed to more financial liability now that the Supreme Court has imposed homosexual "marriage" across the country, David French wrote in National Review.

Pastors are reaching out to their insurance companies inquiring whether their liability insurance will cover them should they be sued for refusing to perform a homosexual "marriage," and so far, the answer is not good.

"We have received numerous calls and e-mails regarding the Supreme Court's ruling on same-sex marriages. The main concern is whether or not liability coverage applies in the event a church gets sued for declining to perform a same-sex marriage," Southern Mutual Church Insurance Company Vice President of Underwriting David Karns wrote July 1 in an "all states" agents' bulletin.

Southern Mutual covers more than 8,400 churches.
"The general liability form does not provide any coverage for this type of situation, since there is no bodily injury, property damage, personal injury, or advertising injury," Karns told his agents. "If a church is concerned about the possibility of a suit, we do offer Miscellaneous Legal Defense Coverage."

"This is not liability coverage," he clarified, "but rather expense reimbursement for defense costs."

"There is no coverage for any judgments against an insured," he wrote.

"In other words," French wrote, "Churches, you're on your own."

It is unusual for an insurer to deny completely hypothetical claims, French added. Normally, coverage decisions are made only after evaluating the claims in the complaint and the policy terms.

Lawsuits and fines against individual bakers, florists, photographers and others for refusing to provide services for homosexual "weddings" are stacking up across the U.S.

The Oregon Bureau of Labor and Industries recently assessed a $135,000 fine against Christian bakers for refusing to bake a wedding cake for a lesbian couple. (The state said the refusal caused the homosexuals "emotional, mental and physical suffering.")

French said that so far there are no meaningful judicial precedents that would permit interference with churches' core First Amendment rights to this degree, but "lawsuits challenging church liberties are inevitable."

The Iowa Civil Rights Commission having declared that discrimination bans on the basis of sexual orientation and gender identity "sometimes" apply to churches and has also stated that a "church service open to the public" is not a "bona fide religious purpose" that would limit the law's application.

Further, a New Jersey administrative-law judge ruled in 2012 that a religious organization "closely associated with the United Methodist Church" wrongly denied access to its facilities for a homosexual "wedding."

The lawsuits over homosexual "marriage" up to this point have demonstrated that going forward litigants are very likely to allege that they suffered "personal injury" if a church refuses to perform or host their wedding ceremony, he said.

For example, the lesbian couple in the Oregon bakery case claimed a long list of injuries which included "impaired digestion," "high blood pressure," "excessive sleep," "migraine headaches," and "anxiety."

These allegations were over a mere cake, a cake they were able to instantly replace, French pointed out, not the entire wedding.

Although churches can find first-rate pro bono counsel, legal non-profits do not and cannot indemnify a church's potential liabilities, said Senior Legal Counsel with the Alliance Defending Freedom (ADF) Erik Stanley.

That's what insurance is for.
Even though other insurers contacted for the story had not yet made statements to their insureds similar to that of Southern Mutual, one had posted a legal analysis of Obergefell v. Hodges and included guidelines for avoiding litigation.

Stanley focuses a substantial amount off his practice on defending religious-liberty rights for pastors and churches.

Asked the real-life effect of Southern Mutual's decision, he replied, "More fear."

https://www.lifesitenews.com/news/churches-that-refuse-to-perform-gay-marriages-may-lose-insurance-coverage

End

12 - PUBLIC SERVICE CAMPAIGNS

Kenneth Cole Creates and Launches "We All Have AIDS" Public Service Campaign on World AIDS Day

www.psaresearch.com

"More than two decades into the worst healthcare crisis the world has ever known, stigma still challenges efforts to prevent, to treat and, ultimately, to cure HIV/AIDS. Together with a persistent lack of access to testing, care and treatment, stigma means that 90% of the people living with HIV/AIDS don't know it. But by joining forces, we can prevent, control and eradicate stigma. That is what the "We All Have AIDS" campaign is about. Because if one of us has AIDS, we all have it."

Celebrities and leaders in the fight against HIV/AIDS join forces with Cole, Viacom and the Kaiser Family Foundation to help erase stigma

Kenneth Cole, in conjunction with KNOW HIV/AIDS, a joint public education initiative of Viacom Inc. and the Kaiser Family Foundation, unveiled the "We All Have AIDS" campaign, which brings together key entertainment, political, social and scientific leaders in an effort to foster needed solidarity and to bring light to the devastating stigma associated with those living today with HIV/AIDS.

The campaign goal is to encourage millions to learn more, protect themselves, get tested and find treatment. The effort includes an arresting photograph with a compelling message about stigma that will be seen and heard by hundreds of millions via newspaper, magazines, radio and outdoor public service advertisements (PSAs), along with a new dedicated website, a t-shirt initiative and public art installation.

The campaign exemplifies a unified response to the HIV/AIDS epidemic, asserting that if anyone has AIDS, we all do, and if it exists anywhere it essentially exists everywhere.

"Our goal is to create the largest public service campaign in the history of the devastating HIV epidemic. After two decades, stigma still challenges efforts to prevent, treat and to ultimately cure HIV/AIDS. This coalition represents many of the world's most accomplished, devoted and inspiring AIDS activists. With help from these extraordinary role models we hope to foster solidarity so that the world can focus on improving HIV prevention and treatment programs, and support necessary AIDS research," says Kenneth Cole.

As part of the campaign's collaboration with KNOW HIV/AIDS, the outdoor PSAs ran across Viacom's outdoor properties, including billboard, bus and bus shelter advertising faces in the nation's largest markets. Radio spots feature Richard Gere, Barry Manilow, Ben McKenzie, Liza Minnelli, Julianne Moore, Natasha Richardson and Mena Suvari, among others, who lend their voices and read the "We All Have AIDS" tagline aloud. These spots will air on a number of Viacom's 179 Infinity Broadcasting radio stations, a majority of which are located in the top 50 markets.

"For the past three years, KNOW HIV/AIDS has brought together the power of our media brands and Kaiser's expertise to spark a dialogue about the devastating effects of AIDS," said Carl D. Folta, Executive Vice President of Viacom. "Kenneth Cole, too, has been at the forefront of raising AIDS awareness, and we believe the combined power of these shared visions will bring a new level of urgency to the epidemic proportions this disease has reached."

In addition, the "We All Have AIDS" print PSAs ran in about 200 publications internationally, including Vogue, French Vogue, Vanity Fair, Bell' Italia, Luna, InStyle, InStyle Spain, The New Yorker, The Sunday Telegraph, Elle Belgique, Men's Journal, Out, Us Weekly, Time, People, Rolling Stone and many others. The six-page insert will also run on World AIDS Day in The New York Times, Boston Globe, and The Chicago Tribune.

"Uniting such a powerful, high-profile group sends a strong and clear message that HIV/AIDS is an issue that deserves the world's attention and more still needs to be done," said Matt James, Senior Vice President, Kaiser Family Foundation.

Kenneth Cole has also created a website that allows users to learn more about the disease and other HIV/AIDS organizations, some of which are supported by the featured participants. Additional information is available at another website where users can locate a nearby HIV testing site and find more information on ways to get involved in the fight.

Limited edition "We All Have AIDS" t-shirts were sold at Barneys New York stores, Kenneth Cole New York stores, Theory New York stores, Scoop New York, Planet Blue in Los Angeles and Louis Boston in Boston. Holt Renfrew in Canada and Selfridges in London will also carry the t-shirts.

The proceeds from the $35 t-shirt will go to the "We All Have AIDS" foundation to help further promote solidarity and the eradication of the stigma of AIDS through prevention and education programs.

About "We All Have AIDS"
More than two decades into the worst healthcare crisis the world has ever known, stigma still challenges efforts to prevent, to treat and, ultimately, to cure HIV/AIDS. Together with a persistent lack of access to testing, care and treatment, stigma means that 90% of the people living with HIV/AIDS don't know it. But by joining forces, we can prevent, control and eradicate stigma. That is what the "We All Have AIDS" campaign is about. Because if one of us has AIDS, we all have it."

https://www.psaresearch.com/kenneth-cole-creates-and-launches-we-all-have-aids-public-service-campaign-on-world-aids-day/

End

13 – LBGTQ STRATEGY - RELENTLESS PRESSURE

Major LGBT Group Urges Biden to Strip Accreditation of Christian Schools, Colleges

ChristianHeadlines.com

Michael Foust | Contributor

November 19, 2020

The nation's largest LGBT advocacy group, the HUMAN RIGHTS CAMPAIGN [HRC] is urging the future Biden administration to help pull the accreditation of Christian colleges and schools if they don't have a policy prohibiting discrimination based on sexual orientation and gender identity. The Human Rights Campaign posted its goals for the Biden administration in a Nov. 11 document, Blueprint for Positive Change. The 22-page brief includes dozens of objectives for the Biden White House, but its targeting of Christian institutions would have a major impact on religious schools.

Under a current law known as the Higher Education Opportunity Act, accrediting agencies are told to ensure their standards "respect the stated mission of the institution of higher education," including a school's "religious" mission.

HRC, in its blueprint, says the language "could be interpreted to require accrediting bodies to accredit religious institutions that discriminate or that do not meet science-based curricula standards."

The Department of Education, HRC says in its blueprint, "should issue a regulation clarifying that this provision ... does not require the accreditation of religious institutions that do not meet neutral accreditation standards including nondiscrimination policies and scientific curriculum requirements."

Albert Mohler, president of Southern Baptist Theological Seminary in Louisville, Ky., calls such a recommendation "sinister."

"I've not seen any document like this before – the Human Rights Campaign is effectively calling for religious colleges and schools to be coerced into the sexual revolution or stripped of accreditation," Mohler said this week in a column and on his Briefing podcast. "... In terms of accreditation, that is an atomic bomb.

A Direct Threat to Christian Education—The Human Rights Campaign Demands...

The accreditation of Christian colleges and schools has just been directly targeted by the nation's most influential LGBT advocacy group...

"In clear text, for all the world to see, the Human Rights Campaign summons the Biden administration to deny accreditation – or, at the very least, to facilitate the denial of accreditation – to Christian institutions, Christian colleges and universities, and, for that matter, any other religious institution or school that does not meet the demands of the LGBTQ orthodoxy. This would mean abandoning biblical standards for teaching, hiring, admissions, housing, and student life. It would mean that Christian schools are no longer Christian."

Mohler called it an "open threat to the ability of Christian colleges and schools to operate by Christian conviction."

"This is an outright attempt to eliminate religious freedom for Christian schools – or for any religious school that refuses to bow to the moral revolutionaries at the Human Rights Campaign," he said. "... This is an undisguised attempt to shut down any semblance of a Christian college or university that would possess the audacity to operate from a Christian worldview."

The complete text of Mohler's Letter:

"This is an outright attempt to eliminate religious freedom for Christian schools – or for any religious school that refuses to bow to the moral revolutionaries at the Human Rights Campaign," he said. "... This is an undisguised attempt to shut down any semblance of a Christian college or university that would possess the audacity to operate from a Christian worldview."

A Direct Threat to Christian Education—The Human Rights Campaign Demands that the Biden Administration Deny Accreditation to Christian Colleges and Schools

The accreditation of Christian colleges and schools has just been directly targeted by the nation's most influential LGBTQ organization. The Human Rights Campaign has recently issued a document directed at the incoming administration entitled Blueprint for Positive Change 2020. The Blueprint demands that President-elect Biden adopt a legislative agenda and enact specific executive orders that are in line with the LGBTQ movement—a movement that Biden pledged to champion.

Contained within its pages are perhaps some of the most alarming demands that threaten religious liberty, and the mainstream media has given little to no attention to this dimension of the report.

The Blueprint is not ambiguous—it makes detailed policy positions and recommendations, department by department, for the Biden Administration to deploy once the president-elect assumes office. From the Department of Agriculture to the Department of Health and Human Services, the Human Rights Campaign demands the enactment of policies to prohibit what is identified as discrimination.

In the Department of State, for example, the Blueprint urges the department to, "include a non-binary gender marker and modernize existing requirements for updating gender markers on United States' passports." Such policy proposals would upend a system specifically designed to quickly and accurately identify individuals for the purposes of safety and security. Hence this is why, when reporting a crime or a missing person, a police officer will ask you if the suspect or missing person is male or female. Passports are designed for specificity in order to promote safe travel throughout the United States and around the world—a policy likely to be undermined by a passport that includes "non-binary" gender markers and is "modernized" for our cultural moment. All this contributes to the elimination of gender or sex as a meaningful category – which is not accidental. If the intention is to remake humanity, the passport will have to be redefined.

Also included within the recommendations for the Department of State is the following: "Create a panel of human rights experts to review the conclusion of the Commission on Unalienable Rights and provide inclusive recommendations." The Blueprint justifies that policy proposal by arguing, "The Commission on Unalienable Rights was designed to challenge the international consensus with a narrow view to human rights that, among other things, would leave LGBTQ people even more vulnerable to violence and discrimination."

To be clear, the Department of State established the Commission on Unalienable Rights in order to identify those rights that all human beings possess—rights that ought to be recognized for every human being around the world. Those unalienable rights stand contrary to invented and artificial rights that have been declared by various courts around the world.

By calling for the end of this commission, the Human Rights Campaign has levied a veiled critique of the Trump administration's State Department under Secretary of State Mike Pompeo. The Biden administration, according to LGBTQ activists, must correct the missteps of the Commission on Unalienable Rights by reasserting the newly invented sexual liberties of the LGBTQ movement.

Indeed, the Blueprint argues that the Commission was created to "challenge the international consensus" on rights and liberties, especially sexual liberties. The problem with this, however, is that if you are looking for an international consensus on the issue of unalienable rights, you will not find it at the Human Rights Campaign. You will not find an international consensus in the Blueprint. It is intellectually dishonest for this group to claim an international consensus for the LGBTQ revolution—a consensus that, quite frankly, does not exist.

Yet, the most shocking demand in the report is found under the section for the Department of Education. The Human Rights Campaign demands the Biden administration to ensure that "non-discrimination policies and science-based curriculum are not undermined by religious exemption to accreditation standards."

That is sinister. I've not seen any document like this before—the Human Rights Campaign is effectively calling for religious colleges and schools to be coerced into the sexual revolution or stripped of accreditation.

The Blueprint states, "Language regarding accreditation of religious institutions of higher education in the Higher Education Opportunity Act could be interpreted to require accrediting bodies to accredit religious institutions that discriminate or do not meet science-based curricula standards. The Department of Education should issue a regulation clarifying that this provision, which requires accreditation agencies to 'respect the stated mission' of religious institutions, does not require the accreditation of religious institutions that do not meet neutral accreditation standards including nondiscrimination policies and scientific curriculum requirements."

In terms of accreditation, that is an atomic bomb.

In clear text, for all the world to see, the Human Rights Campaign summons the Biden administration to deny accreditation—or, at the very least, to facilitate the denial of accreditation—to Christian institutions, Christian colleges and universities, and, for that matter, any other religious institution or school that does not meet the demands of the LGBTQ orthodoxy. This would mean abandoning biblical standards for teaching, hiring, admissions, housing, and student life. It would mean that Christian schools are no longer Christian.

This is insidious from top to bottom. Schools that will not get in line with the moral revolution, if the Biden Administration acts as demanded, will be denied their accreditation. We must not miss the language: Accreditation should be revoked for those who do not meet the LGBT "non-discrimination" standards or "science-based curricula standards."

Wait just a minute. The Human Rights Campaign is not known for any particular agenda on the creation-evolution front, nor is the group preoccupied with particle physics. The Human Rights Campaign is targeting issues of sexual orientation and gender identity, cloaking them in the language of "science." This is an undisguised effort to require Christian schools and colleges to abandon biblical authority or lose accreditation.

This is an open threat to the ability of Christian colleges and schools to operate by Christian conviction.

This is an outright attempt to eliminate religious freedom for Christian schools—or for any religious school that refuses to bow to the moral revolutionaries at the Human Rights Campaign.

If the Human Rights Campaign achieves its policy goals, religious institutions will either be coerced into capitulation over fundamental religious and theological doctrines, or they will be marginalized. This kind of policy goes even further than, for example, attempts to strip federal funding and student aid from institutions that will not surrender to the LGBTQ movement. Indeed, accreditation is a more basic and pervasive threat—those colleges or universities would not be permitted to participate in the GI Bill; students would not be allowed to transfer their credits nor would they be allowed to apply for graduate study at other institutions. The threat to accreditation is more basic than the threat to federal funding. It would threaten even institutions that do not receive a single penny of government funding.

This is an undisguised attempt to shut down any semblance of a Christian college or university that would possess the audacity to operate from a Christian worldview. This comes with chilling specificity and clarity. We dare not miss what is at stake."

https://www.christianheadlines.com/contributors/michael-foust/major-lgbt-group-urges-biden-to-strip-accreditation-of-christian-schools-colleges.html

Human Rights Campaign

From Wikipedia, the free encyclopedia

www.hrc.org

The Human Rights Campaign (HRC) is the largest LGBTQ advocacy group and political lobbying organization in the United States.[2] The organization focuses on protecting and expanding rights for LGBTQ individuals, most notably advocating for same-sex marriage, anti-discrimination and hate crimes legislation, and HIV/AIDS advocacy. The organization has a number of legislative initiatives as well as supporting resources for LGBTQ individuals.

Structure

HRC is an umbrella group of two separate non-profit organizations and a political action committee: the HRC Foundation, a 501(c)(3)[3] organization that focuses on research, advocacy and education; the Human Rights Campaign, a 501(c)(4)[4] organization that focuses on promoting lesbian, gay, bisexual, transgender, and queer (LGBTQ) rights through lobbying Congress and state and local officials for support of pro-LGBTQ bills, and mobilizing grassroots action amongst its members; and the HRC Political Action Committee, a super PAC which supports and opposes political candidates.[5]

Leadership

The Human Rights Campaign's leadership includes President Alphonso David.[6] HRC's work is supported by three boards: the Board of Directors, which is the governing body for the organization; the HRC Foundation Board, which manages the foundation's finances and establishes official policies governing the foundation; and the Board of Governors, which manages the organization's local outreach nationwide.[7]

History

Human Rights Campaign headquarters in Washington, D.C.

Steve Endean, who had worked with a previously established Gay Rights National Lobby from 1978, established the Human Rights Campaign Fund political action committee in 1980.[8] The two groups eventually merged. In 1983, Vic Basile, at the time one of the leading LGBT rights activists in Washington, D.C., was elected as the first executive director. In October 1986, the HRC Foundation (HRCF) was formed as a non-profit organization.[9]

In January 1989, Basile announced his departure, and HRC reorganized from serving mainly as a political action committee (PAC) to broadening its function to encompass lobbying, research, education, and media outreach.[10] HRC decided on a new Statement of Purpose: "For the promotion of the social welfare of the gay and lesbian community by drafting, supporting and influencing legislation and policy at the federal, state and local level." Tim McFeeley, a Harvard Law School graduate, founder of the Boston Lesbian and Gay Political Alliance, and a co-chair of the New England HRC Committee, was elected the new executive director. Total membership was then approximately 25,000 members.[11]

In 1992, HRC endorsed a presidential candidate for the first time, Bill Clinton. In March 1993, HRC began a new project, National Coming Out Day. From January 1995 until January 2004, Elizabeth Birch served as the executive director of the HRC. Under her leadership, the institution more than quadrupled its membership to 500,000 members.[12]

In 1995, the organization dropped the word "Fund" from its name, becoming the Human Rights Campaign. That same year, it underwent a complete reorganization. The HRC Foundation added new programs such as the Workplace Project and the Family Project, while HRC itself broadly expanded its research, communications, and marketing/public relations functions. The organization also unveiled a new logo, a yellow equal sign inside of a blue square.[13]

The Human Rights Campaign often has a large presence at LGBT-related events such as the Chicago Pride Parade as seen above.

As part of the activities surrounding the Millennium March on Washington, the HRC Foundation sponsored a fundraising concert at Washington, D.C.'s RFK Stadium on April 29, 2000. Billed as a concert to end hate crimes, "Equality Rocks" honored hate crime victims and their families, such as featured speakers Dennis and Judy

Shepard, the parents of Matthew Shepard. The event included Melissa Etheridge, Garth Brooks, Pet Shop Boys, k.d. lang, Nathan Lane, Rufus Wainwright, Albita Rodríguez, and Chaka Khan.[14][15]

Elizabeth Birch's successor, Cheryl Jacques, resigned in November 2004 after only 11 months as executive director. Jacques said she had resigned over "a difference in management philosophy".[16]

In March 2005, HRC announced the appointment of Joe Solmonese as the president. He served in that position until stepping down in May 2012 to co-chair the Barack Obama presidential campaign.[17]

HRC launched its Religion and Faith Program in 2005 to mobilize clergy to advocate for LGBT people, and helped form DC Clergy United for Marriage Equality, which was involved in the legalization of same-sex marriage in the District of Columbia.[18] On March 10, 2010, the first legally recognized same-sex weddings in the District of Columbia were held at the headquarters of the Human Rights Campaign.[19]

On August 9, 2007, HRC and Logo TV co-hosted a forum for 2008 Democratic presidential candidates dedicated specifically to LGBT issues.[20]

In 2010, HRC lobbied for the repeal of the United States' ban on HIV-positive people's entry into the country for travel or immigration.[21][22]

In September 2011, it was announced that Joe Solmonese would step down as president of HRC following the end of his contract in 2012.[23] Despite initial speculation that former Atlanta City Council president Cathy Woolard would be appointed, no replacement was announced until March 2, 2012, when American Foundation for Equal Rights co-founder Chad Griffin was announced as Solmonese's successor. Griffin took office on June 11, 2012.[24]

In 2012, HRC said that it had raised and contributed $20 million to re-elect President Obama and to advance same-sex marriage.[25] In addition to the Obama re-election campaign, HRC spent money on marriage-related ballot measures in Washington, Maine, Maryland

and Minnesota, and the election of Democratic Senator Tammy Baldwin in Wisconsin.[26]

In 2013, HRC conducted a postcard campaign in support of the Employment Non-Discrimination Act (ENDA).[27]

In 2019, HRC joined with 42 other religious and allied organizations in issuing a statement opposing Project Blitz, an effort by a coalition of Christian right organizations to influence state legislation.[28]

References

[1]"IRS Form 990 FY18" (PDF). Human Rights Campaign. Internal Revenue Service. Retrieved 29 January 2019.

"Democratic hopefuls pressed on gay issues at forum". CNN. August 10, 2007. Retrieved November 9, 2015.

"HUMAN RIGHTS CAMPAIGN FOUNDATION". ProPublica. Retrieved 16 September 2015.

"Human Rights Campaign". OpenSecrets.org. Center for Responsive Politics. Retrieved 16 September 2015.

Leven, Rachel (January 3, 2012). "Human Rights Campaign creates super-PAC". The Hill. Retrieved 16 September 2015.

Simon, Carolyn. "We Will Win: Get to Know New HRC President Alphonso David". Human Rights Campaign. Retrieved 7 August 2019.

"The HRC Story: Boards". hrc.org. Human Rights Campaign. Retrieved August 24, 2012.

[failed verification] Lambert, Bruce (August 6, 1993). "Stephen R. Endean, 44, Founder Of Largest Gay Political Group". New York Times. Retrieved 16 September 2015.

Haggerty, George; Zimmerman, Bonnie (2003). Encyclopedia of Lesbian and Gay Histories and Cultures. Garland Science. p. 710. ISBN 9781135578718.

Birch, Elizabeth (Fall 1995). "The Human Rights Campaign: So Much More Than a Fund". Human Rights Campaign: 2–3. Archived from the original on 2012-02-13.

Bailey, Mark (2000). "Human Rights Campaign." Gay Histories and Cultures. New York: Garland. Archived from the original on 2012-02-13.

Althafer, Emily. "Leading gay rights advocate to speak at UF". University of Florida News: source: Adelisse Fontanet, xxx-1665 ext. 326. Archived from the original on September 16, 2006. Retrieved February 22, 2012.

"The HRC Story: About Our Logo". Human Rights Campaign. Retrieved February 22, 2012.

"More Artists Added to Equality Rocks: Michael Feinstein, Chaka Khan, Kathy Najimy and Rufus Wainwright Join Garth Brooks, Ellen DeGeneres, Melissa Etheridge, Anne Heche, Kristen Johnston, kd lang, Nathan Lane and Pet Shop Boys To Benefit the Human Rights Campaign Foundation". nyrock.com World Beat. Archived from the original on November 15, 2012. Retrieved February 22, 2012.

"Resources: Hate Crimes Timeline". Human Rights Campaign. Retrieved February 22, 2012.

Seelye, Katharine (December 1, 2004). "Gay Advocacy Group Says Its President Is Resigning". New York Times. Retrieved 15 September 2015.

"Joe Solmonese Named Human Rights Campaign President: Leader with Unmatched Record to Embark on Heartland Tour during First Week on Job". Human Rights Campaign. March 9, 2005. Retrieved February 22, 2012.

Stewart, Nikita (December 18, 2009). "Fenty to sign same-sex marriage bill at church in NW D.C". The Washington Post.

Marimow, Ann E.; Alexander, Keith L. (March 10, 2010). "First gay marriages in District performed". The Washington Post.

ABC News. "Dems Court the Gay Vote". ABC News.

"After 22 Years, HIV Travel and Immigration Ban Lifted". Human Rights Campaign. Retrieved February 22, 2012.

"HRC: After 22 years, HIV travel and immigration ban lifted - Steve Rothaus' Gay South Florida". typepad.com.

Chris Geidner (August 27, 2011). "HRC's Solmonese to Step Down, Sources Say No Replacement Has Been Selected". Metro Weekly. Archived from the original on February 29, 2012.

Andrew Harmon (March 2, 2012). "Chad Griffin Named President of HRC". The Advocate. Archived from the original on March 4, 2012.

"HRC 2012: Unprecedented Mobilization for Equality". Archived from the original on February 2, 2013. Retrieved March 8, 2013.

Martel, Ned (November 8, 2012). "Gay rights advocates welcome Election Day results for a change". The Washington Post. Retrieved March 8, 2013.

Eilperin, Juliet (October 25, 2013). "Cindy McCain petitions husband to back gay rights bill". The Washington Post. Retrieved 3 November 2014.

[28] "Statement from 43 National Organizations United in Opposition to Project Blitz and Similar Legislative Efforts" (PDF). Americans United for the Separation of Church and State. Archived from the original (PDF) on 4 February 2019. Retrieved 4 February 2019.

https://en.wikipedia.org/wiki/Human_Rights_Campaign

End

14 – PURSUING THE COURT SYSTEM IN THE EPISCOPAL CHURCH AND THE FEDERAL COURTS

Five diocesan conventions voted to withdraw from the Episcopal Church: the Diocese of San Joaquin, the Diocese of Fort Worth, the Diocese of Quincy, the Diocese of Pittsburgh, and the Diocese of South Carolina. This did not include individual congregations that have also withdrawn, as in the Diocese of Virginia where members of eight parishes voted to leave the Episcopal Church. Included were the historic Falls Church and Truro Church. These congregations then formed the Anglican District of Virginia, which became part of the Convocation of Anglicans in North America (CANA).

The first diocesan convention to vote to break with the Episcopal Church was the Episcopal Diocese of San Joaquin. On December 8, 2007, the convention of the Episcopal Diocese of San Joaquin voted to secede from the Episcopal Church and join the Anglican Province of the Southern Cone, a more conservative and traditional member of the Anglican Communion located in South America. A minority of parishes and individuals reorganized the diocese and remained in the Episcopal Church. The Superior Court of California ruled July 18, 2009, that the diocese could not leave the Episcopal Church and that their acts were void. Those who remained in the Episcopal Church gained control of the property.

The convention of the Episcopal Diocese of Pittsburgh also voted to leave the Episcopal Church and join the Province of the Southern Cone. This split occurred after the House of Bishops deposed Robert Duncan from office in September 2008.

In 2008, the Diocese of Quincy in Illinois and the Diocese of Fort Worth voted to leave the Episcopal Church. The convention of the

135

Diocese of Fort Worth, under the leadership of Jack Leo Iker, and with the vote of 80 percent of the voting clergy and laity, also voted to align with the Province of the Southern Cone. In response to the departure of Iker and the Fort Worth diocese, Presiding Bishop Schori falsely declared that Iker had "abandoned the communion" and joined with the local diocese in suing Iker and followers, to reclaim church buildings and property.

Two years later the Episcopal Diocese of South Carolina declared that an earlier vote by their Standing Committee was now in effect and that they had left the Episcopal Church. The Diocese then held a special convention in November 2012 to affirm that action. However, Bishop Lawrence and his followers did not immediately join the Anglican Church of North America and remained a free-standing diocese. They then sued in South Carolina Courts, claiming they were doing so to protect their property. The court ordered those staying in the Episcopal Church to refrain from calling themselves the Diocese of South Carolina.

Bishop Schori criticized these moves and falsely claimed that schism is not an "honored tradition within Anglicanism" and schism has "frequently been seen as a more egregious error than charges of heresy" for there has been schism in the churches for centuries. Schism actually grows the Church; with new church bodies being formed by the spin off members.

Those remaining in the Episcopal Church were wrongly recognized immediately by the Presiding Bishop and executive Council of the Episcopal Church as the continuation of the old diocese.

Church Property Litigation

In 1993, the Connecticut Supreme Court concluded that former parishioners of a local Episcopal church could not keep the property held in the name of that parish because it found that a relationship existed between the local and general church such that a legally enforceable trust, the Dennis Canon, created by TEC, existed in favor of the TEC over the local church's property.

In December 2008, a Virginia trial court ruled that eleven congregations of former Episcopalians could keep parish property when the members of these congregations split from the Episcopal Church to form the Anglican District of Virginia. The Episcopal Church claimed that the property belonged to it under the canon law of the Episcopal Church after appeals reached the Virginia Supreme Court, a new trial was ordered which resulted in a decision returning the property to the Episcopal Church. Subsequent appeals by those who had left the Episcopal Church were unsuccessful including an appeal by one parish to the U.S. Supreme Court in 2014.

Other rulings in Colorado and California ordered congregations that have voted to change their associations within the Anglican Communion to return their properties to the Episcopal Church. On January 5, 2009, the California Supreme Court ruled that St. James Anglican Church in Newport Beach could not keep property held in the name of an Episcopal parish. The court concluded that even though the local church's names were on the property deeds and legally recorded among the land records for many years, the local churches had agreed to be part of the general church, and thus in effect voided ownership. A lazy bench indeed, they did not want to get involved with church matters. A huge mistake, for this was an ownership of property matter. And just like that the Vestries lost their own churches, altars, pews, candles and all.

Property litigation in Pittsburgh began before the split when Calvary Episcopal Church filed suit against Duncan in 2003 in order to ensure diocesan property remained in the Episcopal Church. A second parish, St. Stephen's in Wilkinsburg later joined Calvary as a plaintiff. This resulted in a signed stipulation specifying that diocesan property would remain the property of the Episcopal Diocese of Pittsburgh in the Episcopal Church U.S.A.

In 2009, the Judge of the Court of Common Pleas ruled that the 2005 agreement signed by Duncan to settle the Lawsuit brought by Calvary Church meant that diocesan property belonged to those remaining in the Episcopal Church. This was confirmed in January 2010 with a decision including a schedule of property to be returned. The group that left changed its name to the Anglican Diocese of Pittsburgh but appealed the decision. In 2011, a panel of judges from the appellate court in Pennsylvania affirmed that ruling, and the full appellate court declined to review the ruling. The state Supreme Court also declined to hear an appeal. The Anglican Diocese of Pittsburgh announced that it would not pursue further appeals.

The Dennis Canon prevailed in the Federal Court system almost in every Lawsuit with the exception of two cases in Ft. Worth Texas and South Carolina.

The Canon I.7.4 reads as follows:

"All real and personal property held by or for the benefit of any Parish, Mission or Congregation is held in trust for this Church and the Diocese thereof in which such Parish, Mission or Congregation is located. The existence of this trust, however, shall in no way limit the power and authority of the Parish, Mission or Congregation otherwise existing over such property so long as the particular Parish, Mission or Congregation remains a part of, and subject to, this Church and its Constitution and Canons."

"….So long as the particular Parish, Mission or Congregation remains part of. And subject to, this Church and its Constitution and Canons."

What needs to be said here is what this dispute did to the Laity or members of the Episcopal Church. It broke their hearts. It broke their hearts to see and witness their Episcopal Church file civil lawsuits against their own Dioceses and Parishes, Bishops, Priests, Vestries, and Clergy.

The Laity of those Parishes of course were devastated, not one of them expected this to happen to their congregation. Involved in a civil lawsuit by their own Church? That would never happen they thought, but it did.

The Presiding Bishop, acting through her Chancellor's law firm, and various bishops initiated litigation of over seventy secular lawsuits against dioceses, parishes, clergy, and volunteer vestry members seeking to depart with parish property to which they hold title. These lawsuits include sixteen states: California, Colorado, Connecticut,

Florida, Georgia, Illinois, Massachusetts, Nebraska, New York, Ohio, Pennsylvania, South Carolina, Tennessee, Texas, Virginia, and Wisconsin.

Litigation is not how Christians resolve conflicts with each other. Presiding Bishops in the past have not acted litigiously and settled matters peacefully.

In 1873, Bishop George Cummings of Kentucky and Reverend Charles Cheney of Chicago met in New York City and with a number of clergy and laity left TEC to establish the Reformed Episcopal Church (REC).

Two fellow denominations, the Presbyterian and Lutheran Churches, allowed parishes and clergy to depart with their property. In 1973, many presbyteries (similar to dioceses) in the Presbyterian Church in the United States (PC-USA) allowed parishes to leave to found the Presbyterian Church in America (PCA). Inquiry to the national PCA office did not reveal any litigation over property. Last year, 2012, the Pittsburgh Presbytery publicly announced that parishes wishing to leave can do so after negotiation. In the Evangelical Lutheran Church of America (ELCA) one hundred ninety-nine (199) parishes left in 2010 to form a new Church body. One hundred thirty-six (136) other Lutheran churches await a second required vote of convention to leave peacefully. In light of this comparative information, the litigious policy by the Presiding Bishop is out of step with that of other mainline denominations.

There can be little doubt that most Episcopalians are deeply troubled by this litigation and want TEC to put an end to the madness of Christians suing Christians and wasting millions of dollars of church funds. The parishioners and clergy departing TEC are not mean-spirited people in an "organization who wants to put us out of business" as the Presiding Bishop reportedly said. To the contrary, they are fellow Christians who are faithful people acting out of Christian conscience.

The American Anglican Fellowship Trustees filed a letter of possible charges with the Episcopal Church Court system on December 18, 2013 seeking to resolve these issues that were dividing the church. Citing violations of the Constitutions and Canons by Presiding Bishop Katherine Jefferts Schori. The letter of possible charges to Bishop Matthews follows:

"The American Anglican Fellowship Inc. (AAF) believes it necessary to post this letter because a leaked copy is currently circulating the Internet. We regret this happening however, to insure accuracy and the purpose and intent of AAF action, the following is a true copy of the AAF letter dated 12/19/2013 reporting possible violations of the Constitution and Canons by the Presiding Bishop of the Episcopal Church sent to the Intake Officer. Hyperlinks refer to published public reports and articles. None of the published reports or articles used as information to the Intake Officer is confidential or privileged, neither civil or criminal, but ecclesiastical in nature. The public articles and reports referred to in this letter are not necessarily the opinion of AAF Inc.

AAF understands the Intake Officer will perform a preliminary investigation to determine if the information is true, it would or would not, constitute a violation of the Title IV Disciplinary Canons. We await his decision.

American Anglican Fellowship Inc.
P.O. Box 434
Brandywine, MD 20613
December 19, 2013

Dear Bishop Matthews,

The American Anglican Fellowship, Inc. (AAF), an organization of current and former members of The Episcopal Church (TEC), submits this Information to you regarding possible violations of the Constitution and Canons by the Presiding Bishop in accordance with Canon IV.6.2 and with the understanding that, "by virtue of Baptism, all Members of the Church are called to holiness of life and accountability to one another" (Canon IV.I).

Many Episcopalians believe TEC has departed from the traditional faith held by the consensus of the Anglican Communion and world Christendom. To remain in unity with the "one holy catholic and apostolic church" (Nicene Creed, John 17:21-23, 1 John 1:3), some transfer to another Anglican body (e.g., Anglican Church in North America) or to another denomination. Some parishes have departed TEC with their properties after diocesan negotiations. However, in the vast number of situations, the Presiding Bishop and various bishops (her assigns) have filed lawsuits to seize these properties and taken action to extinguish TEC clergy from the ordained ministry who have transferred to another Anglican Church.

A petition by more than 5,000 Christians, including 697 clergy and 24 bishops, unsuccessfully sought to obtain an explanation from the Presiding Bishop concerning the litigious actions that have squandered an estimated $21.5 million in Church funds – money that should be used for traditional Christian purposes.

The litigation and punitive administrative actions are a discredit to all as they contradict (1) Christ's teaching to be charitable and loving towards fellow Christians (Mt. 5:43-48); (2) apostolic instructions not to sue other Christians (1 Cor. 6:1-7); (3) policies of past Presiding Bishops allowing parish departures with property; and (4) practices of other denominations (e.g., Presbyterian and Lutheran). When the Israelites were called by God to leave Egypt, they were allowed to leave with their property (Ex. 12:31-36). TEC should do nothing less. Pharaoh's attempt to get the Israelites and property back had disastrous consequences. The same can happen to TEC. With departing parishes, TEC should have the spirit of Gamaliel -- if it is God's will, these parishes and TEC may someday re-unite (Acts 5:38-39). In the Civil War, TEC split between North and South. After the war, parishes and dioceses re-united.

Title IV, "Ecclesiastical Discipline," establishes procedures whereby Members of the Clergy "shall be subject to proceedings" for "knowingly violating or attempting to violate, directly or through the acts of another person, the Constitution or Canons of the Church or of any Diocese" (Canon IV.3.1(a)). Members of the Clergy "shall be accountable for any breach of the Standards of Conduct set forth in Canon IV.4" when they are "material and substantial" or "of clear and weighty importance to the ministry of the Church" (Canon IV.3.2-3).

A number of public reports and articles have been issued over the past few years describing conduct alleged to violate TEC's Constitution and Canons. Based on this information and belief, descriptions of six alleged offenses are provided below.

First Offense

Based upon information and belief, the Presiding Bishop violated and continues to violate (1) Canon IV.19.2 by seeking interpretation of TEC canons by secular courts, and (2) Canon IV.4.1 (e) which requires the safeguarding of TEC property and funds

Public reports indicate that the Presiding Bishop, acting through her Chancellor's law firm, and various bishops have initiated (or continued) litigation of over seventy secular lawsuits against dioceses, parishes, clergy, and volunteer vestry members seeking to depart with parish property to which they hold title. These lawsuits include sixteen states: California, Colorado, Connecticut, Florida, Georgia, Illinois, Massachusetts, Nebraska, New York, Ohio, Pennsylvania, South Carolina, Tennessee, Texas, Virginia, and Wisconsin.

Over forty of the lawsuits involve actions against parishioners who voluntarily served as vestry members or other leadership positions. In some cases, the Presiding Bishop and various bishops are seeking personal assets of these parishioners for monetary punitive damages causing undue and unjust personal financial hardship and mental suffering to them. The current estimated cost for TEC litigation exceeds $21.5 million. This estimate would be even higher if it included the money spent by individual dioceses participating in the litigation and that of parishes, dioceses, clergy and lay people being sued by TEC.

Litigation is not how Christians resolve conflicts with each other. Presiding Bishops in the past have not acted litigiously and some diocesan bishops do not wish to act this way today.

In 1873, Bishop George Cummings of Kentucky and Reverend Charles Cheney of Chicago met

in New York City and with a number of clergy and laity left TEC to establish the Reformed Episcopal Church (REC). Research on this event did not reveal any administrative charges or litigation over property by TEC. Today, some dioceses have allowed clergy and parishes to leave to join another Anglican body or the Roman Catholic Church. (e.g., parishes in Dallas, Kansas, and Washington left with property and a Maryland parish without property). Press reports and other sources indicate the Bishop of Virginia, with tacit approval from the former Presiding Bishop, were negotiating a departure of over seven parishes seeking to leave TEC with their property. After the new Presiding Bishop's election, negotiations ceased, and litigation began.

Two fellow denominations, the Presbyterian and Lutheran Churches, have allowed parishes and clergy to depart with their property. In 1973, many presbyteries (similar to dioceses) in the Presbyterian Church in the United States (PC-USA) allowed parishes to leave to found the Presbyterian Church in America (PCA). Inquiry to the national PCA office did not reveal any litigation over property. Last year, 2012, the Pittsburgh Presbytery publicly announced that parishes wishing to leave can do so after negotiation. In the Evangelical Lutheran Church of America (ELCA) one hundred ninety-nine (199) parishes left in 2010 to form a new Church body. One hundred thirty-six (136) other Lutheran churches await a second required vote of convention to leave peacefully. In light of this comparative information, the litigious policy by the Presiding Bishop is out of step with that of other mainline denominations.

The litigation authorized by the Presiding Bishop and various bishops asks courts to interpret provisions of the Constitution and Canons. The litigation thus violates Canon IV.19.2, which provides that "No member of the Church, whether lay or ordained, may seek to have the Constitution and Canons interpreted by a secular court, or resort to a secular court to address a dispute arising under the Constitution and Canons, or for any purpose of delay, hindrance, review or otherwise affecting any proceeding under this Title." The litigation further violates Canon IV.4.1(e), which requires the Presiding Bishop and various bishops, as members of the Clergy, to "safeguard the property and funds of the Church and Community." The expense for litigation is a violation of the canon since other solutions with substantially less cost have been used in the past and today by TEC and by the Presbyterian and Lutheran Churches. For failure to safeguard the property and funds of the Church, the Presiding Bishop "shall be accountable" (Canon IV.4.2). The lawsuits are listed in a publicly released document here.

Second Offense

Based upon information and belief, the Presiding Bishop violated and continues to violate Canon IV.4.1 for misuse of the Abandonment of Communion canons by charging numerous bishops, priests, and deacons with Abandonment for transferring to another Anglican body

According to a 2010 report issued by the American Anglican Council (AAC Report), the Presiding Bishop and various bishops abused the Abandonment of Communion canons for four Bishops and hundreds of priests and deacons who transferred from TEC to another church in the Anglican Communion.

If the Presiding Bishop and various bishops wished to remove TEC clergy from ordained rank status, the AAC report indicates the appropriate canons would be IV.1 and IV.5. These canons call for a trial or other hearing, with confrontation of witnesses and the presentation of both sides of a case. Traditionally, the Abandonment of Communion canons apply to situations where there has been a full departure of a clergy person from TEC and the Anglican Communion. The revised 2012 canons specify "the Church" rather than "this Church" which makes the traditional view more explicit. "The Church" is broader and apparently applies to the Anglican Communion or the "whole Church" (BCP 328-329)

By misuse of the canons, the Presiding Bishop and various bishops extinguished the right of the clergy to exercise the gifts and spiritual authority conferred in ordination at the Anglican Church body where they have transferred. Recognizing the harshness of this action, TEC replacement Bishops in the Dioceses of Pittsburgh and South Carolina lessened the Abandonment charge to "restrict [the] exercise of ministry" only within TEC.

The misuse of the Abandonment of Communion canons by the Presiding Bishop and various bishops violates Canon IV.4.1 (g) that requires her to exercise her ministry "in accordance with applicable provisions of the Constitution and Canons of the Church."

Third Offense

Based upon information and belief, the Presiding Bishop violated and continues to violate

Canons III.12.7, III.7.8, III.9.8 and IV.4.1 (g) by abusing the Renunciation, Release and

Removal canons by claiming "implied renunciation" of numerous bishops, priests, and deacons when written renunciation is required.

According to the same AAC Report, the Presiding Bishop and various bishops wrongfully implied "renunciation" or "release and removal" for nine bishops and hundreds of priests and deacons in the absence of specific written declarations of renunciation required by Canons III.12.7, III.7.8, and III 9.8. In these cases, the bishops, priests and deacons transferred to another church in the Anglican Communion and informed the Presiding Bishop they had not renounced their orders.

The most glaring misuse involves Bishop Henry Scriven, ordained and consecrated in the Church of England by the Archbishop of Canterbury. Bishop Scriven was not in fact a Bishop of "this Church" as required by the canon the Presiding Bishop invoked when she purported to remove him from the ordained ministry and to pronounce him "deprived of the right to exercise the gifts and spiritual authority as a Minister of God's Word and Sacraments conferred on him in Ordinations." He was serving as an Assistant Bishop in the Diocese of Pittsburgh. TEC's Presiding Bishop had no authority to deprive Bishop Scriven of the ministry conferred on him in the Church of England. Bishop Scriven had notified the Presiding Bishop of his transfer back to the Church of England to become an Honorary Assistant Bishop of the Diocese of Oxford subject to the jurisdiction of the Bishop of Oxford where he would work as director of a missionary society of the Church of England. Yet, the Presiding Bishop removed him from the ministry—or at a minimum, barred him from TEC.

Abuse of the renunciation, release and removal Canons III.12.7, III.7.8 and III.9.8 violates Canon IV.4.1 (g) that requires the Presiding Bishop to exercise her ministry "in accordance with applicable provisions of the Constitution and Canons of the Church."

Fourth Offense

Based upon information and belief, the Presiding Bishop violated Canons IV.3.1(a), IV.4.1(h)(8), and I.17.8 by unconstitutionally assuming power to remove members and dissolve a lawfully existing Standing Committee under Canon 1.17.8

Based upon public reports and an article issued by the Anglican Communion Institute, Inc. (ACI), the Presiding Bishop violated Canon IV.3.1 (a) with an unconstitutional assumption of power in removing members of the Standing Committee for the Diocese of San Joaquin and dissolving that lawfully existing Standing Committee through misuse of Canon I.17.8. The Constitution and Canons do not grant the Presiding Bishop authority to remove any one from office.

From the ACI article, AAF understands that in 2006, the San Joaquin Diocesan Convention voted to withdraw from TEC to join the Anglican Communion Province of the Southern Cone. The Standing Committee, however, planned to keep the diocese in TEC and operate the diocese under TEC's Constitution and Canons. The Standing Committee President informed the Presiding Bishop of this intent. Nonetheless, the Presiding Bishop notified the President and Standing Committee that she no longer recognized it, dissolved the Committee, and called a Special Convention for the diocese.

Without Canonical authority under Canon I.17.8, the Presiding

146

Bishop dissolved a lawfully constituted Standing Committee and appointed another. She also called a Special Convention to bypass the lawfully existing Standing Committee in the appointment of an Interim Bishop. Both actions appear to be an unconstitutional assumption of power in violation of Canon IV.3.1(a) and Canon IV.4.1(h)(8) for "Conduct Unbecoming a Member of the Clergy.

Fifth Offense

Based upon information and belief, the Presiding Bishop may have violated Canons IV.4.1(g) and IV.4.1(h)(8) by harassing Clergy and Abusing Disciplinary Procedures

Based upon news reports and a Religion News Service article, in 2011 and 2012, nine bishops submitted affidavits or a friend of court brief in pending litigation involving the Dioceses of Quincy and Fort Worth where they basically stated that the ultimate authority of TEC is the diocese. AAF understands that the Presiding Bishop and various bishops caused disciplinary action against the nine bishops that resulted in their agreement to an Accord.

In the Religion News Service article, it cited one bishop who said, "All nine of us are processing some degree of anger and are feeling substantially alienated from those who brought the charges against us . . . We feel alienated and victimized. We are nowhere near happy about this outcome, even though we stand by our decision to accept the Accord." In contrast, there was no objection to twenty-nine bishops who filed a friend of court brief in a secular court in 2013 stating a position contrary to the consensus of the Anglican Communion (of which TEC is a "constituent member"). That consensus is represented by 1998 Lambeth Resolution I.10, the "whole church" (BCP 328-329), and the mainstream interpretation of Scripture on the subject.

The disciplinary proceedings against the nine bishops can intimidate other clergy from expressing their expert views. An Accord with the bishops was reached, but that does not necessarily mean there was no undue pressure on the bishops or whether they were treated equally with other bishops who have made other filings in secular courts.

For these reasons, the disciplinary action taken against the nine bishops for filing positions in courts may be a violation of Canon 4.1(h)(8) for "Conduct Unbecoming a Member of the Clergy" and Canon IV. 4.1(g) for not exercising her ministry in accordance with "Community rule" within the community of bishops. AAF believes these bishops should have a right to believe that if they file a friend of court brief in a secular court, they will all be treated equally with other bishops according to fundamental fairness.

Sixth Offense

Based upon information and belief, the Presiding Bishop wrongfully (1) claimed that a bishop of South Carolina had abandoned communion with TEC and (2) established a replacement bishop and diocesan machinery to operate the diocese, both of which violated Canons IV.3.1(a), IV.4.1(h)(8), and IV.16(A).

Based upon news reports and an Open Letter to the Bishops by the Anglican Communion Institute (ACI) dated November 27, 2012, with "Appendix: A Comprehensive Assault on a Diocese," the Presiding Bishop wrongfully caused Abandonment of Communion charges to be made against the Bishop of South Carolina when the Bishop was keeping the diocese "intact and in TEC."

The ACI Letter reported that "The evidence is overwhelming that [TEC] violated canons and engaged in discussions deceitfully. We disagree with those who accept the evidence but think the matter inconsequential. If our leaders will not follow the canons and formal procedures of the church, not only in letter but in spirit, they forfeit any trust they may hold and undermine the mutual trust of the church as a whole. We disagree with those who think that such disregard of letter and spirit is merited by the misbehavior of [the Bishop of South Carolina]. Canonical violation and deceit will never produce peace in the church or render a just outcome."

As indicated by the ACI Letter to the Bishops, these actions violate (1) Canon IV.3.1(a) for "knowingly violating or attempting to violate, directly or through the acts of another person, the Constitution or Canons of the Church or of any Diocese;" (2) Canon IV.4.1(h)(8) for

"Conduct Unbecoming a Member of the Clergy," and (3) Canon IV.16(A) which requires for Abandonment of The Episcopal Church (i) "an open renunciation of the Doctrine, Discipline or Worship of the Church [not this Church – see Second Offense];" (ii) "formal admission into any religious body not in communion with the same;" or (iii) "exercising Episcopal acts in and for a religious body other than the Church or another church in communion with the Church."

Request for Action

An immediate investigation is requested of these reported violations to determine whether this information, if true, constitutes offenses that should be forwarded to the Reference Panel (Canon IV.6.4-10). The secular lawsuits are continuing. One lawsuit was filed by the Diocese of Chicago as recently as November 6, 2013. There can be little doubt that most Episcopalians are deeply troubled by this litigation and want TEC to put an end to the madness of Christians suing Christians and wasting millions of dollars of church funds. The parishioners and clergy departing TEC are not mean-spirited people in an "organization who wants to put us out of business" as the Presiding Bishop has reportedly said. To the contrary, they are fellow Christians who are faithful people acting out of Christian conscience, and they should not be subject to wolves in the Episcopate (Mt. 7:15)

Faithfully Submitted,

The American Anglican Fellowship Inc.

By its Trustees

Episcopal Church's Hit List Against Orthodox Clergy Tops 700 and Counting

www.virtueonline.org

By David W. Virtue and Mary Ann Mueller

July 16, 2013

Bishop Charles von Rosenberg When Provisional Bishop Charles von Rosenberg of the Episcopal Church in South Carolina (TECinSC) released his list of 103 Episcopal Diocese of South Carolina clergy who could be cut from the clerical rolls and sliced from their pensions and health insurance, The Episcopal Church passed an infamous number ... 700.

VOL has documented more than 700 cases of Episcopal clergy - mostly priests, a few deacons and at least a dozen bishops - who have been uncanonically inhibited, deposed, and or released from their ordained ministries as they valiantly strive to remain faithful to the Gospel even as The Episcopal Church disintegrates into spiritual decay and temporal anarchy.

Early Depositions

Little by little, the list of inhibited and deposed clergy grows - a list which first began in 1977 when two priests, a continent apart, were relieved of their Episcopal priesthood and ministry by their respective bishops.

In April 1977, the Episcopal News Service reported that the Rev. Robert S. Morse at St. Peter's Episcopal Church in Oakland, California was inhibited and would be eventually deposed by California Bishop Kilmer Myers, claiming that the priest had voluntarily abandoned the ministry of The Episcopal Church.

Bishop Myers is quoted as saying that he acted with "great personal pain and anguish" in inhibiting Fr. Morse and setting up the

150

mechanism by which he would be deposed. The bishop also counseled the faithful not to receive any sacraments from the priest.

"No loyal Episcopalian or Anglican may receive the sacraments from the Rev. Robert Morse," the bishop is quoted as saying in the ENS story.

Robert Sherwood Morse would later become the Archbishop of the Anglican Province of Christ the King (APCK), a continuing Anglican Church body.

On the East Coast, the Rev. Canon Albert J. duBois found himself in the crosshairs of Long Island Bishop Jonathan Sherman. For 24 years, Canon duBois was executive director of the American Church Union. As such he stood up in the 1976 General Convention and challenged the passage of the resolution that allowed the ordination of women to the Episcopal priesthood and noted that the unprecedented action "placed the Episcopal Church outside the traditional doctrine, discipline, and worship of Anglicanism."

The Canon charged that Convention "acted unconstitutionally in attempting to give permission for the ordination of women to the priesthood". For his clarion call to The Episcopal Church, duBois was rewarded with inhibition and later deposed by his bishop and charged with "forming a new church."

Canon duBois became the international president of Anglicans United. He stated that the "threatened deposition was simply an effort to single him out in order to crush any organized opposition to the Minneapolis actions."

Canon duBois reported that there were "over one hundred separatist congregations" in the U.S. He predicted there would be "over two hundred and fifty such congregations by the end of 1977, with many more in 1978."

In August of 1977, five Episcopal priests in the Diocese of Los Angeles and one in the Diocese of Colorado were deposed as they opposed the approval of the ordination of women to the priesthood brought on by the 1976 General Convention of the Episcopal Church.

The priests -- supported by their congregations -- had renounced the authority of their bishops.

Earlier in June of that year, Bishop William C. Frey of Colorado deposed the Rev. James Mote of St. Mary's Episcopal Church in Denver, the first of a number of parishes and missions to vote to sever relations with its Episcopal diocese in opposition to the ordination of women.

In August, Bishop Robert C. Rusack of Los Angeles deposed the Rev. John Barker and the Rev. Elwood Trigg of St. Mary of the Angels Church, Hollywood; the Rev. William T. St. John Brown of St. Matthias, Sun Valley; the Rev. Forrest Miller of Our Savior's, Los Angeles; and the Rev. George H. Clendenin of the Church of the Holy Apostles, Glendale.

Since those early Episcopal Church actions against traditionalist priests, many clergy have felt the ecclesiastical weight and animosity of their bishops and standing committees whenever their orthodox views clash with the revisionist theology of The Episcopal Church that has actively embraced liberal theology and aligned itself with contemporary culture and American society. Their loyalty to Christ and His Church and to the "faith once for all delivered to the saints" has been rewarded with their ministries being torn out from under them, or at least on paper.

VIRGINIA

Bishop Peter James Lee

Bishop Peter James Lee removed 21 clergy from ordained ministry in 2007 claiming they had abandoned the Communion.

The bishop explained that the former Episcopal clergy were "released from the obligations of priest or deacon and deprived of the right to exercise the gifts and spiritual authority conferred in ordination."

Of the 21clergy deposed, one Virginia priest recanted and returned to TEC fold. A 2007 ENS report said the Rev. Nicholas Lubelfeld "has declared his loyalty to the doctrine, discipline and worship of The Episcopal Church" as a result Bishop Lee lifted Fr. Lubelfeld's inhibition and returned him to full ministry in the Episcopal Diocese of Virginia.

FLORIDA

Bishop Samuel Howard

By 2008 Florida Bishop Samuel Johnson Howard had deposed 42 orthodox Episcopal priests.

When he first took office, Howard seemed the picture of sweet reasonableness, promising to work with everyone, his door open to all, announcing that he was orthodox as he followed in the footsteps of the late evangelical Bishop of Florida, Steve Jecko.

In January 2004, things looked promising when the Diocese of Florida decided to uninvite Presiding Bishop Frank Griswold for the much-anticipated consecration of Howard as the next Bishop Coadjutor of Florida. There was an air of euphoria, a general feeling then that the change from Bishop Jecko to Howard would be a transition that orthodox priests could live with. They soon became disillusioned.

Thus began his ecclesiastical reign of terror. He was not gospel driven, but showed himself to an institutionalist, a corporatist, obedient not to those who paid his bills in the diocese, but as the CEO of a diocese whose boss resided at 815 2nd Avenue, New York, a city with which he was all too familiar.

For the orthodox clergy of the diocese, the joy quickly turned into disillusionment when it became clear that Howard had adopted the party line and would not go against the liberal Episcopal House of Bishops or his uber boss, Frank Griswold and, later, Katharine Jefferts Schori.

When seven orthodox priests in his diocese requested alternative pastoral oversight, Howard bluntly said no, that he would only entertain Delegated Episcopal Pastoral Oversight (DEPO). The Rev. Kurt Dunkle, Canon to the Ordinary blasted their actions as political. The seven parishes appealed to the Archbishop of Canterbury's Panel of Reference but got nowhere.

The formation of the Anglican Alliance in November 2001, at the urging of Bishop Jecko, gave form and shape to orthodoxy in the diocese. At that time, most of the clergy and laity in the Diocese of Florida were supportive of the traditional orthodox beliefs of the church while watching as the leadership of the Episcopal Church USA turned its back on many of the doctrines that are central to that belief. Their mission was to try to turn the tide of theological revisionism back to the solid foundation of the traditional faith once delivered to the saints.

By the end of 2003, it became evident that the Episcopal Church would not heed the cries from within the American church, or from the worldwide leadership of the Anglican Communion, to turn back from its trajectory towards theological innovation.

SAN JOAQUIN

Bishop Jerry Lamb.

A few Clergy from an entire departing diocese were deposed at once as the orthodox diocese realigned with another province within traditional Anglicanism. In May 2009, Provisional Bishop Jerry Lamb deposed a total of 61 active and retired clergy in the (TEC) Diocese of San Joaquin by charging the central California clergy with "Abandonment of the Communion."

The San Joaquin clergy were given six months to 12 months to recant their position, renounce their orders, or deny charges of abandonment.

"The fact is, they chose to abandon their relationship with The Episcopal Church," Bishop Lamb said. "They declined to ask for a release from their ordination vows, and I had no option but to bring the charges of Abandonment of the Communion ..."

FT. WORTH

Provisional Bishop Wallis Ohl.

In February 2010, just as the Anglican Church in North America was being established in Bedford, Texas, the remaining (TEC) Fort Worth diocese, loyal to The Episcopal Church handed down a letter

154

deposing 57 clergy charging them with violating Canon IV.10.1, the Abandonment of Communion of The Episcopal Church. The letter was signed by the second Provisional Bishop of TEC Fort Worth, Wallis Ohl.

PITTSBURGH

Bishop Bob Duncan.

Those remaining in the TEC Diocese of Pittsburgh were kinder to nearly 100 Anglican clergy who followed their Bishop Robert Duncan as he forged out in the deep seeking to remain loyal to Christ through realigning with the Southern Cone. Eventually, his herculean efforts resulted in the creation of the Anglican Church in North America, an emerging Anglican province. In October 2009, Pittsburgh's realigning clergy were simply released from "their ministerial ties to The Episcopal Church so that they can become licensed in any entity they choose."

The TEC Pittsburgh action was seen as a pastoral solution by the diocesan standing committee. At the time, Bishop Keith Price had not yet been made Pittsburgh's provisional bishop.

"We're doing this for pastoral reasons," said the Rev. Dr. James Simons, the TEC diocesan standing committee president. "We do not want to see our priestly brothers and sisters deposed."

QUINCY

Bishop John Buchanan

A month earlier, in September 2009, the Provisional Bishop of TEC Quincy deposed 34 priests and deacons, claiming that they had renounced their ministries in The Episcopal Church and declaring that those clergy are now deprived of all the authority conveyed in ordination.

"We did leave The Episcopal Church. We did not renounce our ordination vows, or abandon our ministries," commented Fr. John Spencer, president of the Anglican Diocese of Quincy Standing Committee. "The supposed inhibitions and depositions of our clergy have no bearing on those clergy, or on their ministries, since our diocese is no longer under the authority of the Episcopal Church. The actions of Episcopal Bishop John Buchanan simply mean that The Episcopal Church no longer wants these clergy to be allowed to function in any of their churches."

WESTERN NEW YORK

Bishop Michael Garrison.

In October 2009, The Episcopal Bishop of the Diocese of Western New York, J. Michael Garrison deposed four priests and two deacons from St. Bartholomew's Anglican Church, Tonawanda. A letter dated Sept. 19th said that the Revs. Arthur Ward, Jr., John E. Commins, Richard Molison as well as Deacons Edward Kaczmierek and John Reitz had abandoned the communion of The Episcopal Church and were now formally deposed. All three priests and two deacons deny they have abandoned the Communion of the church and are now under the authority of the Anglican Church in North America.

Sometimes Episcopal clergy were deposed one at a time or in clusters of two or three or in small groups. These inhibitions and depositions are scattered throughout several dioceses of The Episcopal Church including, but not limited to: Atlanta, Colorado, Connecticut, East Carolina, Florida, Indianapolis, Kansas, Kentucky, Los Angeles, Massachusetts, Michigan, Milwaukee, Mississippi, New Jersey, Newark, New York, North Carolina, Oklahoma, Pennsylvania, Rio Grande, Rochester, San Diego, Southern Virginia, Tennessee and West Tennessee.

SOUTH CAROLINA

Bishop von Rosenberg.

The most recent mass inhibitions of Episcopal clerics -- some 103 -- came at the hands of the Provisional Bishop of the Episcopal Church in South Carolina. Bishop von Rosenberg and the TEC in SC Standing Committee meted out the action on July 10.

"If there is no response from the restricted clergy in 60 days, the canons require the Bishop to remove them from the ordained ministry," a news release from The Episcopal Church in South

Carolina (TECinSC) reported. To date, there are 88 clergy who are keeping their clerical ties with The Episcopal Church.

AMERICAN ANGLICAN COUNCIL

In February 2010, the American Anglican Council released a document in which it was able to track the clerical status of 404 Episcopal priests and deacons and 12 bishops who have been inhibited, deposed, or released by the Episcopal Church national headquarters at 815 Second Avenue in New York.

However, those figures did not include the 100 or so Pittsburgh clergy, the 57 deposed from Fort Worth, another 27 clergy from Quincy and 10 more from San Joaquin who were not included in the original list, nor the 103 clerics pushed out in South Carolina inching the true figure to 700 or more. This may be a conservative figure when all the depositions are individually counted.

AAC Chief Operating Officer Canon Phil Ashey explained that trying to get an exact figure on the number of Episcopal clergy who have been axed by The Episcopal Church is a hard thing to do.

"Well-it [the figure] is a moving target which changes weekly," he told VOL, "because we are compiling the numbers of those who are leaving by one's, two's and three's every week."

Many of the deposed clergy are remembered on AAC's Wall of Honor. Canon Ashey was deposed by Virginia Bishop Lee in December 2005.

"Yes, we do have our 'Wall of Honor,' on which we post the framed letters of Deposition," explained Canon Ashey, who proudly displays his own Letter of Deposition on the Wall of Honor. "You can imagine the names on that wall-- including most of the leaders of ACNA today. It is truly a Wall of Honor - TEC has been responsible in large part for creating ACNA."

End

Mary Ann Mueller is a journalist living in Texas. She is a regular contributor to VirtueOnline

https://virtueonline.org/episcopal-churchs-hit-list-against-

American Anglican Fellowship Issues Open Letter to Episcopalians to end Unjust Lawsuits

March 30, 2015

"By virtue of Baptism, all Members of the Church are called to holiness of life and accountability to one another. The Church and each Diocese shall support their members in their life in Christ and seek to resolve conflicts by promoting healing, repentance, forgiveness, restitution, justice, amendment of life and reconciliation among all involved or affected." Episcopal Church USA Canon IV.1

The American Anglican Fellowship (usanglicanfellowship.com), a group of long-time current and former members of the Episcopal Church, took this canon very seriously when we filed a Complaint against Presiding Bishop Katherine Jefferts Schori in December 2013. The Episcopal Church is in civil court spending more than $40 million in 84 lawsuits against their member Dioceses and Churches. Over forty of the lawsuits involve actions against parishioners who voluntarily served as vestry members or other leadership positions. In some cases, the Episcopal Church is seeking personal assets of these parishioners for monetary punitive damages causing undue personal financial hardship. AAF asked why is the Church in civil courts when they are charged by their own Canon "to resolve conflicts by promoting healing, repentance, forgiveness, restitution, justice, amendment of life, and reconciliation among all involved or affected"?

Secondly, more than 700 departing clergy were deposed in this conflict which "bars them from ministry not only in the Episcopal Church in the United States, but also in the world-wide Anglican Communion." Recognizing the harshness of this action, the Dioceses of Pittsburgh and South Carolina graciously lessened the charges. The Diocese of Pittsburgh informed "scores of priests that they can be released from their ministerial ties to the Episcopal Church to become licensed in any entity they choose." In a letter from the Diocesan Standing Committee, the clergy were given an option of stating their desire to remain active in the Episcopal Church or to allow the release to proceed. "We're doing this for pastoral reasons," says the Rev. Dr. James Simons, the Standing Committee president. "We do not want to see our priestly brothers and sisters deposed."

AAF believes that total reconciliation of this conflict is impossible for we now have two churches under one roof, but conciliation between the two sides in the conflict is definitely achievable. The AAF also believed the Laity had to act through some sort of a formal complaint, for several letters to the Presiding Bishop went unanswered. A petition http://tinyurl.com/pqxw3ma signed by more than 5,000 Christians requesting clarity and information of the dispute was abruptly dismissed by two church lawyers citing "the litigation money was well spent, for the value in property received was far in excess of money spent." A shocking response to say the least; had they considered the big picture outside of the monetary gains, they would have found 1.5 million Episcopalians had either left for another Anglican Church, another denomination, or left the Christian faith altogether; and more than 500 Episcopal Churches had closed their doors.

The AAF complaint http://tinyurl.com/p5dc7xo was generated from hundreds of published articles of the lawsuits and reports of violations of the Church Constitution and Canons. The stories of persons involved in this conflict are heartbreaking. There is pain and suffering on both sides of the aisle, long time friendships are destroyed; and good clergy are being denied their rights of Ordination. These unjust acts have forever changed thousands of lives and destroyed relationships in our churches. There are so many persons, clerical and laity, who have been damaged by these actions it is impossible to determine the actual harm that has come to them. Every AAF Trustee actually experienced this tragedy in their home parish in the Washington Diocese.

The AAF submitted its complaint on December 29, 2013. The preliminary investigation was performed by the Intake Officer and completed in July 2014. He dismissed all six charges.

AAF respectfully disagreed with the Intake Report and promptly appealed. The Appeal is still being reviewed by the President of the Disciplinary Board.

Whether the charges are, or are not violations of the Constitution and Canons, the AAF's stated primary interest is that we saw the entire complaint process as an opportunity for a pastoral resolution of the issues that divide Episcopalians. AAF filed its complaint based on the revised Title IV Canons that placed an "emphasis on pastoral resolution" rather than a criminal justice model, reflecting "more clearly on the theology of the Episcopal Church." AAF provided information not to persecute or defame anyone, but to initiate a possible resolution of conflicts.

Litigation is not how Christians resolve conflicts with each other. Some Diocesan Bishops negotiated a peaceful settlement with those parishes and clergy wishing to depart prior the Presiding Bishop's intervention http://tinyurl.com/cleeblt ending negotiations. Other denominations have also allowed parishes and clergy to depart with their property. In 1973 the Presbyterian Church in the United States allowed parishes to leave to found the Presbyterian Church in America (PCA). In 2012, the Pittsburgh Presbytery publicly announced that parishes wishing to leave can do so after negotiation. In 2010, the Evangelical Lutheran Church of America 199 parishes left to form a new Church body. One hundred thirty-six (136) other Lutheran churches await a second required vote of convention to leave peacefully. In light of this comparative information, the litigious policy of the Episcopal Church is out of step with that of other mainline denominations where peaceful conciliation was reached.

This madness of this church-inflicted pain and suffering to its members must stop, and there is an opportunity at the General Convention on June 25-July 3, 2015 in Salt Lake City, Utah. The Convention can end these unprecedented and unjust lawsuits and acts with an appropriate Resolution to begin a process of conciliation for all parties affected, satisfactory to all.

AAF specifically calls for the Convention to execute a Resolution to end these lawsuits and allow those Dioceses, Parishes and Clergy wishing to depart from the Episcopal Church, to leave with their property after negotiations at the diocesan level. Further recognizing that the departing are members in good standing and supporting their quest to transfer to another Anglican Church body and become recognized members of the Anglican Communion if they so desire; and restoring all rights and privileges of ordination of the 700 deposed or suspended clergy.

We urge all Episcopalians to join this effort and contact your Deputies to General Convention http://www.generalconvention.org/deputations to prepare a resolution to end this conflict. It is the right thing to do.

Faithfully,

The American Anglican Fellowship, Inc. by its Trustees

End

The Right Reverend William Love
An Orthodox Diocesan Bishop is forced to step down.

The Rt. Rev. William Love told the 152nd meeting of the Diocese of Albany synod that he will step down from office as bishop effective 1 February 2021. The announcement was made during his presidential address to the diocesan convention on 24 Oct 2020.

He stated in his presidential address:

As I reported to the Diocese on October 5th, the Hearing Panel has found me guilty of failing to abide by the Discipline and Worship of the Episcopal Church, and thus violating my ordination vows. They issued a 42-page document outlining their decision, a copy of which has been posted on the Diocesan Website.

The Summary of Opinion outlining the Panel's report, states: "This Panel unanimously concludes that TEC has met its burden of showing, by clear and convincing evidence, that Bishop Love has violated Canon IV.4.1(c) in that his November 10, [2018] Pastoral Directive violated the Discipline of the Church, as Resolution B012 was properly constituted and passed as an authorized revision to the BCP as expressly provided for in Constitution Article X, thus requiring that all Bishop Diocesans permit their clergy the option to utilize such rites. TEC has further met its burden of establishing that Bishop Love's Direction also violated the Discipline of the Church in that it violated Canon I.18. The canonical legitimacy of Resolution B012 rendered Canon I.18 mandatory, requiring adherence by Bishops Diocesan in permitting their Clergy the option to perform same-sex marriage rites. TEC has also met its burden of establishing that the Direction violated the Worship of the Church in that Resolution B012 added canonically-authorized same-sex marriage rites to the Worship of the Church pursuant to BCP."

As I shared in my October 5th communique to the Diocese, I am very disappointed and strongly disagree with the Decision of the

Hearing Panel, particularly their belief that I violated my ordination vows and their argument that B012 was passed as an authorized revision to the Book of Common Prayer. The Episcopal Church's case against me, hinged on their interpretation of the nature of B012. Was it properly constituted and passed as an authorized revision to the Book of Common Prayer (BCP) or not?

It is my belief and that of my legal team that B012 was presented as an alternative resolution to one which would have changed the BCP. It was intended to ensure that same-sex marriages would be allowed in every Diocese, regardless of the Diocesan Bishop's theological views regarding marriage, while at the same time not changing the 1979 Prayer Book.

With that said, while I don't agree with the Hearing Panel's ruling, they have issued their judgement. Unfortunately, given the nature of this case, and the Episcopal Church's demonstrated intent to ensure all dioceses (where civil law permits) allow for same-sex marriages, I have no reason to believe that appealing the Hearing Panel's Decision would result in any different outcome.

A second meeting of the Hearing Panel under the leadership of Bishop Knisely, was scheduled for this coming Monday, October 26th, to determine what disciplinary action should be taken against me. After much thought and prayer, recognizing that whatever disciplinary action would be offered would not be anything I could in good conscience agree to, I have made the very difficult, but necessary decision to resign as Bishop of Albany, effective February 1, 2021 – the 14th Anniversary of my becoming the Bishop Diocesan. Given all that has happened, and that which was still to come, I believe that to stay any longer would be more of a detriment to the Diocese than a help.

The Most Rev. Michael Bruce Curry, Presiding Bishop of The Episcopal Church and I, the Rt. Rev. William H. Love, Bishop of Albany voluntarily entered into an Accord which became effective October 21, 2020, with the unanimous approval of the Disciplinary Board of the House of Bishops. The Accord resolves the matter of my case, thus discharging any further action from the Hearing Panel.

The Accord stipulates the following: I will resign as Bishop Diocesan of the Diocese of Albany, effective February 1, 2021; I will begin a one month terminal sabbatical beginning January 1, 2021; I agree to continue to abide by the January 11, 2019 Restrictions placed upon my ministry by the Presiding Bishop until the effective date of my resignation as Bishop; I will work with the Presiding Bishop through the Office of Pastoral Development to help foster a healthy transition from my leadership as Bishop Diocesan, as the Diocese begins a new chapter in its history; and lastly, I acknowledge that upon February 1, 2021, the effective date of my resignation as Bishop Diocesan, my November 10, 2018, Pastoral Directive regarding B012 will lose force. Until then, however, it remains in effect.

End

Another injustice done by the church of exclusion.

Goodbye good Bishop and Godspeed,

From your faithful servants.

Federal Courts

Don't Panic: The Supreme Court Is Not Going To Overrule Its Same-Sex Marriage Decision

www.forbes.com

Evan Gerstmann Senior Contributor

October 10, 2020

I am a professor and publish on constitutional and educational issues.

The media has lately been awash with dire warnings that "Same-sex marriage [is] at risk as Supreme Court gets more conservative." Two events have triggered this panic. The first is President Trump's nomination of Judge Amy Coney Barrett to serve on the Supreme Court. She is a conservative Catholic. Based on a letter to the Synod Fathers in Christ that she signed, it appears she personally opposes same-sex marriage.

The other cause for concern is a statement recently signed by the Court's two most conservative Justices that sharply criticizes Obergefell v. Hodges, which is the Court's opinion holding that there is a constitutional right to same-sex marriage. Both these concerns are overblown. Judge Coney Barrett hasn't written any judicial opinions on LGBTQ issues. The letter she signed to the Synod Fathers does say that "marriage and family founded on the indissoluble commitment of a man and a woman—provide a sure guide to the Christian life." But that doesn't mean that she plans to foist her ideas of how to live a Christian life on all Americans. The letter also says that marriage is "indissoluble," but no one is writing that she will ban divorce. (The Supreme Court has held that the right to divorce is constitutionally protected.)

But let's say that she does turn out to be a Justice who slavishly applies conservative Catholic teachings to the Constitution. That hardly means that there are now five votes to overturn the Obergefell case. Justices Clarence Thomas and Samuel Alito, the two justices who wrote the statement criticizing Obergefell, are by far the two most conservative Justices on the Court as measured by Martin-Quinn scores. Justices Neil Gorsuch, Brett Kavanaugh, and Chief Justice John Roberts are far closer to the political center than they are.

Tellingly, none of them joined the statement criticizing Obergefell. Indeed, all three of them went along with the Court's decision in that case, which turned away the pleadings of Kim Davis, a religious county clerk who refused to sign same-sex wedding certificates. Davis argued that she is protected by the doctrine of limited immunity and religious freedom. Given that the Court soundly rejected her arguments, it hardly seems likely that one new Justice will so alter the Court's balance that same-sex marriage will be in jeopardy.

Quite the opposite, the current Court appears to be quite friendly to same-sex equality arguments. Last term the Court ruled 6-3 that gay and transgender individuals are protected from discrimination by the 1964 Civil Rights Act. The Court did not have to do that. The justices could have easily held that a statute that prohibits discrimination based on sex does not include protection based on LGBTQ status. The fact that they did so is a strong indication that the Court is not eager to limit the rights of gay and transgender people.

The decision was written by Justice Gorsuch and joined by Chief Justice Roberts. Even with the addition of Judge Coney Barrett, the Court couldn't overturn Obergefell without their votes. While Roberts dissented in the Obergefell case, it is very unlikely that he would vote to overrule it now. He is strongly concerned with the institutional legitimacy of the Court and, in a highly unusual move, publicly rebuked President Trump for implying that there are "Obama judges" and "Trump judges." The last thing he would do is overturn a precedent because Justice Ruth Bader Ginsburg died and was replaced by a Trump appointee.

Also, overturning Obergefell now would create a myriad of problems. What would be the status of all the same-sex marriages that have occurred since Obergefell? What would happen to legally married same-sex couples from other countries who move to America? If same-sex marriage goes back to being a question of state law, what happens to legally married same-sex couples who move to a state that doesn't recognize such marriages? This doesn't seem like the sort of quagmire that the Court would willingly enter in these already challenging times.

Furthermore, even if one thinks of Justices as pure partisans, ending same-sex marriage is hardly a Republican priority. According to Pew Research, more than 60% of Americans support same-sex marriage, including a clear majority of "Republican leaners." Only 37% of Republicans support same-sex marriage, but President Trump has called same-sex marriage a settled issue without provoking any significant backlash. Even if the Court were a strictly partisan institution, which it isn't, this is not the issue the justices would expend political capital on.

As with abortion, the danger is not that the right itself will be overturned, but that the Court will be more tolerant of things that hinder access to that right. The Court ruled in favor of a baker who didn't want to make a cake for a same-sex wedding but did so on extremely narrow grounds. It's possible that the Court may now be more sympathetic to florists, caterers, photographers, and other wedding professionals who don't want to provide their services to a same-sex wedding. But the wedding industry is enormous, so there is little chance that a same-sex couple will be unable to get married due to this sort of refusal of service. It would be a blow to their dignity, and hopefully, the Court won't allow it, but it wouldn't come close to preventing same-sex couples from getting married.

Hopefully, Democratic senators won't focus on this issue during Coney Barrett's confirmation hearings. It would come across as cross-examining her about her religious beliefs, which is exactly how Republicans would like to frame the issue. Democrats would be far better off focusing on the fact that she is being rushed through the confirmation process at a time when Americans have already begun voting for the next president. The public is with them on that issue. The Democrats can't stop her from getting on the Court, but they shouldn't make things worse by implying that a religious person can't separate her personal views from her judicial ones.

https://www.forbes.com/sites/evangerstmann/2020/10/10/dont-panic-the-supreme-court-is-not-going-to-overrule-its-same-sex-marriage-decision/?sh=ed1e112284b9

End

15 - CONCLUSION

Allan S. Haley a dear friend of mine, wrote an excellent article about the Episcopal Church USA in 2008 regarding the demise of the church and their lawsuits suing their own member churches. The article was an excellent analogy of what has happened not only to the Church, but what has happened to our great Nation.

Lawsuits Are a Symptom; the Disease Is Terminal

Allan S. Haley

December 14, 2008

In my legal career, spanning more than 40 years, I can say that I have had experience with more than a thousand lawsuits (that's only an average of two per month---it was probably closer to twice that). In the course of that experience, I have learned a few things about how a lawsuit gets started.

A lawsuit nearly always starts with one party to a dispute taking a position that surprises, angers, and finally provokes the other party into doing something which that other party never intended to do in the first place. Example: you have been living in the same rural home for the last thirty years. You have always reached your home by way of a dirt or gravel road that takes off from a county road and winds its way through three or four other properties before reaching your parcel (and maybe it continues through yours to go on to still more parcels before it dead ends). The neighborhood has settled into a well-known pattern, and everyone is comfortable with the arrangement.

Now one of your neighbors along the road, say one of the ones whose property you have to cross, retires, moves away, or dies---so that his parcel eventually is sold to a new owner. That new owner, say, comes from a fairly large urban or suburban environment, and has dreams of retiring to the country. But no one told him that there were three or four other owners down the road who would be driving through his property twice a day.

Unhappy about having what he sees as his rural peace and quiet disturbed, he consults a surveyor, and learns that there are no recorded easements over the road through his property. So he hires a contractor, puts up big metal gates across the road on each side of his property, and locks them.

You and your neighbors are outraged at having your principal access blocked. (This being the country, there may be an alternative route you can use to get to your home, but it is much less convenient--- perhaps it is very poorly maintained, and floods out during the winter months, or perhaps it takes you way out of your way.) You take a bolt cutter and cut the locks and continue to use the road as before. You probably do not bother to close the gates.

In a week or so, you find special, hardened-steel locks on the gates which your bolt-cutters cannot cut through. At this point, depending on your degree of anger, you either (a) rent a small bulldozer and knock down the gates, or (b) bring a lawsuit. (And if you choose the first alternative, then the owner of the gates starts the lawsuit, and sues you, or has the sheriff arrest you for vandalism.)

Who "started" the lawsuit? As you can see, it is not necessarily the person who filed it. But under the facts I have given, it is easy to pinpoint the action that changed the status quo that had prevailed for over thirty years: it was the decision to block the road by the owner who had just moved in. For better or for worse, he simply assumed he "knew" what the law was and took a position (that the road could not be used by those who were using it) which he assumed the law would support, based on the lack of any recorded easements.

But the law is not so black-and-white. In time, our hypothetical neighbor will learn about "prescriptive rights"---the right to use a road even without a deeded easement. If a person uses someone else's road openly and without asking or receiving permission and continues that use regularly for what the law defines as the "prescriptive period" (in California, it is five years; in other States, it can be ten or even twenty years), then that person acquires a "prescriptive easement" to continue that use, which the law will recognize and protect.

The doctrine of prescriptive easements stems from a social policy that favors the active use and development of land, and discourages passive, absentee ownership. If you live in San Francisco and visit your rural property only once every six months for a week or so, you might never notice the tire tracks that indicate someone else is using your road on a regular basis. And if more than five years go by before you finally find out, you will most likely lose any lawsuit you bring to stop the use.

Now, to the point of this piece: I want to ask, has the prescriptive user "stolen" anything from you? In one sense, of course, he has: he has acquired an easement across your land without having to compensate you for the diminution in value which your parcel will suffer as a consequence of having an easement across it. But in the eyes of the law, you have done the same thing as granting him a deeded easement without charging him for it. The law simply presumes that if five years have gone by without your objecting to the use, or trying to do anything to stop it, you must have no objection to what your neighbor has been doing.

(At this point, let us pause to recall the immortal words of Mr. Bumble in Charles Dickens' Pickwick Papers. When told that the law "presumed" that a wife acts under the direction of her husband, Mr. Bumble replied:

If the law supposes that, . . . the law is an ass—a idiot. If that's the eye of the law, the law is a bachelor; and the worst I wish the law is that his eye may be opened by experience—by experience.

Objecting to what the law "presumes", or "supposes", will not get you very far, as Mr. Bumble learned to his chagrin. In the same way, the landowner who objects to the presumption behind prescriptive rights will receive short shrift from the court.)

All right let's bring the lesson home. As reported on several blogs, the HoB/D Listserv has carried a somewhat extensive debate on the appropriateness of the Episcopal Church (USA)'s spending some $2 million on legal fees in church property disputes over the past year. Those who suggested that the money might have been better devoted to the Church's mission were generally met with argument to the effect that "the ones who are leaving started the lawsuits", or "the departers forced us to sue, because they took the property with them, and it belongs to us." I think I am not being unfair if I summarize the general argument thus:

By canon law [the Dennis Canon], all parish property is held in trust for ECUSA. Therefore, while the members of a parish may choose to leave the Church, they cannot take the property with them---that is theft. Acts of theft leave us with no choice but to file suit. It is the only way the Church can preserve its property for future generations. Thus the $2 million had to be spent, and much more will have to be spent on lawyers before this is over.

Recently, however, facts about the Dennis Canon have emerged which tend to cast the foregoing argument in a slightly different light. For one thing, from what appears in the official records of the 1979 General Convention, the Canon may not have been adopted in the same form by both Houses concurrently, as would be required for it to take effect. And for another thing, it does not appear that the enactment of the Canon was reported to the parishes that were directly affected; the first mention of the Canon in the Episcopal News Service Archives does not occur until 2001---some twenty-one years after its supposed adoption. (I have commented in this post on the disconnect between the deputies elected to General Convention and the parishes that elect them.)

What we have here is a form of "prescriptive right" to parish property that was established in a rush under questionable circumstances, in the waning days of the 1979 General Convention, and then lay dormant for years until a property dispute required its disinterment in 2001. The recognition it has received in some courts in the years since has tended to give it full legitimacy in the eyes of those who invoke it.

But those court decisions simply assumed, without deciding, that the Dennis Canon was a properly enacted provision of Church canon law. The question has now been squarely presented to a trial court in New York, which is one of the States whose highest court has assumed the legitimacy of the Canon heretofore as a given. (Indeed, New York is unique in also having a statute that assumes the existence of the Canon, and purports to legitimize the trust relationship it claims to establish.) No matter what the trial court decides, there is certain to be an appeal; and the question ultimately will have to be decided anew in each State where it arises. Talk about having to fund litigation---just you wait!

Those of you who sympathized with the absentee landowner who woke up one day to find his property subject to an established prescriptive right may now, perhaps, commence to understand why a parish might be surprised to learn that it holds its property in trust for a remote organization who never contributed one penny to either its acquisition or its upkeep. And not only that, but the parish might also well be completely taken aback by the vehemence of those who insist that it is not free to continue to have its name on the deed if it elects to join another diocese---that it forfeits the property in such a case, on pain of being accused of "theft" if it attempts to hold on to it.

I submit that the sudden attempt to adopt the Dennis Canon in 1979, as a knee-jerk reaction to some dictum that had appeared in a decision by the United States Supreme Court just a few months earlier, was the "surprise change in position" by one side to the dispute which set the stage for future lawsuits---every bit as much a surprise as the landowner who suddenly blocks a road that had been used without objection for years. Those who now insist on the "rightness" of their position, based on the assumption that the Dennis Canon indeed was properly adopted in 1979, are no different from that landowner, who came into the midst of a settled neighborhood and decided it was not to his liking, because his property was not entirely under his control. And such a landowner is naive if he believes he can change long-settled expectations suddenly, without notice or negotiation of any kind, and avoid a lawsuit.

In exactly the same way, deputies to General Convention 1979, and the bishops who benefited from the legislation, suddenly (and without any notice or fanfare) changed the centuries-old expectations of the parishes that if they paid for their property and raised the funds to improve it and keep it up for all the intervening years, they and they alone controlled it. Indeed, the very fact that those deputies did not come back and report to each parish what they had done and ensure that they had the parishes' blessing upon and consent to their little canonical change, is for me proof enough that General Convention had already, by 1979, come loose from the moorings which anchored it at the founding of PECUSA just shy of 200 years earlier. And that drift from its moorings is one of the chief factors in the current decline of the Church.

Deputies to General Convention actually brag that they do not represent the parishes and dioceses that elect them---no, indeed, they cannot be bound in that fashion; they must be free to vote as the Holy Spirit guides them, or as their conscience dictates. While such a sentiment might be considered admirable on questions of doctrine and spiritual guidance, it is, I submit, an abomination when it comes to issues of Church property and governance.

The entire early history of PECUSA, which I have sketched at length in this post, is the history of how a solution was found to the problem of uniting sovereign and independent dioceses (State churches) into a national body that suited the new revolutionary character of the United States of America. It could not be an established Church; and no single State church wanted to surrender its sovereign polity---its right to call clergy and to elect bishops, and to meet in diocesan conventions to deal with local matters. From the earliest beginnings of the call for a new national church, there was a strong belief in the principle of subsidiarity, or as the Church in Pennsylvania expressed it, "[t]hat no Powers be delegated to a general ecclesiastical Government, except such as cannot conveniently be exercised by the Clergy and Vestries in their respective Congregations."

A power over the disposition of parish property is precisely the kind of "Power . . . [that can] conveniently be exercised by the Clergy and Vestries in their respective Congregations"---and which therefore could never have been delegated to the national church by those who founded PECUSA. It is all the more important, therefore, that we

176

ask: what has changed in the character of ECUSA that could make the delegation of such a power to the national church appropriate today?

Does the national church contribute any funds at all to the acquisition or maintenance of parish properties? Does it exercise any kind of control over how much is spent on those objects? Does it regulate the design of such churches, or the materials used in their construction? Does it even provide the basis for the property tax exemption which local churches enjoy? The answer to all of these questions, and others similar in nature, is "No." On what basis, therefore, can the national church be said to have any kind of natural claim to local parish property?

There are only two reasons that even remotely come to mind. The first is the one often expressed by the current Presiding Bishop: that such properties "are a legacy . . . for the use of generations [of Episcopalians] yet to come." To which I respond: but is that the Church's actual track record with its property?

Consider the case of this church, or this list of five "closed church properties" in the Diocese of Pennsylvania, with a special assistant in charge of their sale (see the second page, under "Diocesan Staff Changes"). Consider these criteria imposed by the Presiding Bishop on any sale of Church property by a diocese, including a prohibition on their sale to any former congregation that joins another branch of the Anglican Communion. And consider, finally, just how much preservation of property "for future generations" can a Church afford that is unable to replace its aging members with new, younger ones?

Thus spare me, please, the pious talk about "preserving the assets for future Episcopalians." The only other possible justification that can be offered for the Dennis Canon is precisely that which has in fact occurred: it makes it that much more difficult for a given parish to decide to leave the Church. But why should that be a desirable goal for a church? It is nothing but a "dog-in-the-manger" philosophy that says: "We may not be able to use the property if you leave, or keep it on a self-sustaining basis, but we certainly can't let you enjoy it, either." Such a philosophy is all about buildings and property, and not about the people who actually form the essence of a church. It gets the spiritual emphasis exactly backward, and simply exacerbates the emotional trauma of a split. Like a divorcing couple arguing over the community property, it encourages each side to try to use the property as a means to wound or trip up the other, and actually fosters litigation. Thus it is disingenuous in the highest degree for those Episcopalians who back the Dennis Canon to claim that litigation is "forced on them" by those who leave and want to keep their property. It is not those who leave who force ECUSA and its dioceses to bring lawsuits; it is the Dennis Canon itself that does so.

I repeat, nothing in the character of the national Church has so changed in the last hundred years that congregations and their clergy can no longer be trusted with decisions about their local property. Such decisions are routinely made by vestries and clergy month in and month out, with no oversight of any kind from either the diocese or the national church, and matters have been that way ever since the first parish was founded in Jamestown in 1607. The drastic change in these long-standing arrangements attempted with the Dennis Canon must be judged as a ruinous departure from tradition, a failure of leadership and vision that has only increased, and not limited, the fractures visible in the Church today.

I will go further and predict that unless General Convention can be returned to its moorings and be made a body that is responsive to the dioceses and parishes that elect its deputies (at least in matters of property and governance), the disconnect that is presently evident between electors and legislature will enlarge, and eventually engulf the entire Church structure. The budget of General Convention is already unsustainable in a church that is suffering declining attendance and contributions. The budget for lawsuits which its legislation has fostered is out of even General Convention's control, and the Presiding Bishop's decision to have recourse to private slush funds to finance litigation will result in an even larger disconnect between the legislative and the executive branches of the Church. This will, in turn, prove fatal to the Church's central mission.

Thus, all the debate about "inside strategy" versus "outside strategy" is in the end rather academic. There is already forming an "inside" and an "outside" within ECUSA itself: at present, the Presiding Bishop and her staff, along with General Convention, are on the "inside", while the dioceses and parishes that cannot bother even to track what they are doing, or to observe or much less implement the resolutions they adopt, are on the "outside." Meanwhile, the Presiding Bishop is on a course of her own to make her fiefdom a separate and independent "inside" that will inevitably cut off General Convention---which, after all, comes into its Brigadoon-like existence for just two out of every 156 weeks that go by---from any supervisorial function whatsoever, and transform it into an irrelevant body on the "outside" as well.

(A striking example of what I am talking about appeared just yesterday. I would ask that you read and carefully compare two documents available right now on the Web. The first is the Presiding Bishop's letter to the House of Bishops, explaining why she felt it appropriate to declare that the Rt. Rev. Jack L. Iker of Ft. Worth had "voluntarily renounced" his orders in the Church. The second is the written version of the "State of the Diocese" address given by the Rev. Dr. James L. Simons to those wishing to "remain Episcopal" gathered in a special convention in Pittsburgh on December 13. The two documents are only eight days apart in time, but they are light-years apart in perspective. You will readily see that those in Pittsburgh and those at 815 are already speaking different languages and occupying different worlds. It remains to be seen whether Ft. Worth's remnant group will follow Pittsburgh's example, or will allow themselves to be led by 815.)

The ultimate result will be a headquarters at 815 that is completely dependent on wealthy, private supporters, and a General Convention that goes off on whatever activist binges it can manage to scrounge up funding for in the 154 weeks during which it does not meet. The dioceses, meanwhile, will continue on their annual cycles of budgeting and meeting, and their voluntary contributions to 815 will diminish as 815 itself turns more and more to private sources for funding. (Likewise, their contributions to the expenses of deputies to attend General Convention will decline as the deputies increasingly see themselves as independent from the dioceses and look to activist organizations to fund their causes.) In consequence, the dioceses will increasingly have no use for the top-heavy bureaucracy at 815 and will come to view the idealistic and irrelevant activism that characterizes General Convention as a luxury, for which funds are better kept at home.

My point is this: a ship that loses its moorings is ill-equipped to weather a storm. ECUSA has lost its moorings, and there are plenty of storms on the horizon.

End

It's not hard to see that Haley's article, taken from his internet blog fits not only the Episcopal Church, but it fits perfectly with what has happened to America. Read the article again and substitute 'America' for 'The Episcopal Church' and you will see the connection.

Having lived it within the Episcopal Church for 50 years, I saw the connection almost instantly.

Any doubt I had was erased at a Washington Diocesan Convention when a gay priest who was a very vocal leader of Integrity and the rector of a parish on Capitol Hill stood in front of the convention and proclaimed, "We are not only going to bring homosexuality to the church we are going to bring it to the world!" to thunderous applause by the convention delegates.

Note the Capitol Hill location of his parish. Note the Episcopal Church had an office on Capitol Hill. Note also, my bi-sexual rector was involved in the Club on Capitol Hill. How do I know that? His wife told me so.

That was after she tried to take her own life.

The Gay Takeover of America

Town Hall

Crystal Wright

Posted: May 09, 2013

"What is happening to our country? Gays, who represent less than 3% of our population, are trying to dominate our culture and society. Love whom you want. Love the one you're with. People don't really care. This is the message most people want to say but are afraid to because the LBGT (lesbian, bi-sexual, gay and transgender) community will verbally flog anyone who doesn't agree with them. Between gay marriage, gay adoptions, forcing the Boy Scouts to admit gay scouts and scout masters, and lauding a rich NBA player for announcing he's gay, the message is clear from gay America to the 97% of the rest of us. You will accept our lifestyle as mainstream. My response: "No I won't."

Notice when anyone rejects this gay agenda based on religious beliefs or personal views, they are called bigots or mocked. Appearing on Meet the Press May 5, 2013, Republican Newt Gingrich noted the Catholic Church is prohibited from performing adoption services in states like Massachusetts and the District of Columbia because the Church will only allow a married couple (by definition a man and woman) to adopt a baby. This is a perversion of societal norms all in the name of liberals forcing their political correctness down America's throat whether her people have an opinion about it or not.

Liberals are eager to help the "gay lobby" with its takeover of America. The Department of Health and Human Services (HHS) announced March 29, 2013 plans to consider allowing Medicare to pay for sex change surgeries and invited public comments on the topic. Later that day, HHS abruptly pulled the proposal. While the agency said it was due to "an administrative challenge" of Medicare's 1981 decision not to cover such operations, it seems news coverage of HHS' proposal had something to do with its about face. I doubt Republicans in Congress would think sex change operations were a good use of taxpayer money.

There's more. Democratic Senators are pushing to include a "gay couple's" provision in the comprehensive immigration reform legislation. Bowing to the gay strong-arming, Senate Judiciary Chairman Patrick Leahy will offer up the amendment, Uniting Americans Family Act, when the committee votes on the bill. The amendment allows "foreign same sex partners" of legal US residents or citizens to come to America and get a green card. Talk about a target for fraud. What test will the government use to certify people are gay and "permanent partners" and NOT people posing as gay to game the system?

As if the bill didn't have enough problems with its amnesty push for over 11 million criminals and 301 amendments, Senators thought let's make it even more outrageous. Senate Judiciary Chairman Patrick Leahy said he didn't believe the gay partner provision will kill the bill. No, the immigration bill will die a slow death like the Senate's gun bill did because it's mired in mud.

Even though the jobless rate has stayed above 7.5% for the past five years and remains on track to be the longest period of persistent unemployment in 70 years, Democrats want to extend amnesty to as many people possible who aren't even in the US yet. What's next? Allowing relatives of foreign gay partners to come here too? The liberal logic is beyond nonsensical it's downright comical.

No matter how many TV shows are produced about gay couples being married and raising children, or phones calls made by President Obama to gay athletes, homosexuality will never be the majority in our culture. I think it's high time the 97% of the rest of heterosexual America stand up for the preservation of American society not the distortion of it.

https://townhall.com/columnists/crystalwright/2013/05/09/the-gay-takeover-of-america-n1591834

End

This article from 1989 warned of the long-term strategy of the homosexual revolution, including not just same-sex "marriage" but much more.

The Queering of America

NEW AMERICAN

William F. Jasper

Vol. 31, No.14   JULY 20, 2015

The U.S. Supreme Court's decision striking down state laws barring same-sex "marriage" is the culmination of a decades-long corrosive process, one that has been methodically guided by a strategic subversive plan. All moral people are rightly outraged by this official mockery of the natural law, the moral law, and the divine law. But we should not be shocked or surprised, as the unmistakable signs that this was coming have been ever more obvious with each and every concession to the "gay" lobby and "gay" culture. This article originally appeared in the June 8, 1998 issue of The New American, 17 years ago. — The editors

"I want to give you a little more evidence for my notion that this country has shifted in the 1990s and has transformed," lesbian activist Elizabeth Birch told her university audience earlier this year. "Where is the least likely place anybody would look for leadership on a social issue?" she asked. "Corporate America, right?" But therein lies a tremendous irony. Ms. Birch explains: "By 1991, almost no companies in this country, almost none, had even nondiscrimination policies. Just a handful of years later, over half of the Fortune 500 had instituted nondiscrimination policies.... Over 100 of the Fortune 1,500 have instituted domestic partner coverage. That means the CEO at some point says, 'I am going to take on my board, my shareholders, and my customers and do this.' And I've happened to have the privilege to work very closely with a number of these companies. These are household names like Kodak, American Express, IBM, and the Disney Corporation."

Look at Disney

Disney, of course, epitomizes the astonishing transformation of which Ms. Birch spoke. In the past few years, the company once synonymous with wholesomeness and quality family entertainment has become a leading purveyor of perversion — and the target of repeated campaigns by churches and religious organizations offended by its scandalous productions. Who would have thought it possible that the beloved Magic Kingdom would so soon after Walt Disney's passing turn into a Wicked Empire that: hires a convicted child molester to direct a movie; recruits an open lesbian and an avowed homosexual to top executive positions; publishes openly pro-homosexual books directed toward youngsters; injects subliminal pornographic images into its animated movies; produces a children's animated epic with sub rosa homosexual characters; and sponsors an annual homosexual confabulation at Disney World that subjects unsuspecting families to the rowdy and raunchy activities of hordes of deviants?

In her keynote address to the 1998 University of California Lesbian, Gay, Bisexual, Transgendered Association's "Exposed!" conference, Elizabeth Birch triumphantly revealed a deep, dark secret. First, she asked furtively, "Is there any press in the room?" Then she explained: "Okay, I'm gonna tell you — 'cause some of these conversations are very private — but when I said to Michael Eisner, CEO of Disney, [that] '30 percent of your employees are gay,' he said, 'You are wrong, Elizabeth, it's 40 [percent].'"

Until a very short time ago, homosexuality was known as the unmentionable vice. It was not spoken of in decent company. But that recent bygone era seems like ancient history; in "post-Christian America," one cannot open a newspaper, flip a television channel, turn on a radio, watch a movie, or pass a magazine rack without being clobbered by the "gay rights" issue du jour or the latest homosexual-themed pop entertainment offering. An incredible societal transformation — a tectonic shift of enormous magnitude — has taken place before our eyes, in less than the space of one generation. What was once universally seen for the vile abomination that it is, in a few short years has been transmuted into simply a different "lifestyle" or "orientation," protected by law and endlessly defended, glorified, and celebrated by the cultural elites. What was once deviant, abhorrent, and criminal has been rendered by a perverse alchemy into something "polite" society now calls, simply, "gay."

The homosexual revolution is but the latest and most viscerally repellent installment in an ongoing, much larger revolution that has been in the process of upending our entire civilization for many years. And it may yet succeed in doing so. The unimaginable success thus far of the homosexual revolution provides one of the most dreadful portents on the horizon today. For this revolution is far from over. And those "tolerant" citizens who think that, "Hey, I'm not gay, but they're not harming me," have a rude awakening coming. The militant sodomites have made it explicitly clear that tolerance is not sufficient; they demand positive "approval" from society, manifested in the enactment of laws granting them special rights, and the abolition of the residual laws that impede their full homoerotic expression and deny their full access to children. Moreover, as we shall see, they insist on the complete "conversion" of "straight" society, which involves the therapeutic cleansing of all "homophobic," "homohating," "anti-gay bias" attitudes.

Straight America has been asleep on a deadly battlefield with a relentless enemy that is waging total war and believes in giving no quarter. We exaggerate not. In their own words to their own troops, the apostles of perversion describe their lavender jihad as "war" and constantly invoke aggressive, military terms such as "Trojan Horse," "deception," "propaganda," "war strategy," "battle tactics," "hand-to-hand combat," "rage," "fury," "enemy," "war conference," "attack," "hate," "vilify," "destroy," "conquer," "subvert," etc.

"Gay" Agenda

If you are already sickened by the super-saturation of contemporary culture with "gayness" and the non-stop whining about gay victimization, get set for an acceleration of the homo "rights" agenda. The targets include:

• Legalized marriage and adoption rights.

• Mandated "domestic partner" policies for all employers, public and private.

• Vast increases in government funding for all homosexual programs.

• Explicit homosexual "education" at all levels of schooling.

• More homosexual teacher/"role models" in the schools.

• Broad dissemination of explicit homosexual literature in schools and public libraries.

• Abolition of "age of consent" laws.

• Abolition of all state and local statutes restricting homosexual behavior.

• Criminalization, prosecution, and persecution of "homophobes," i.e., religious "bigots."

• A dramatic increase in the visibility of provocative and "diverse" manifestations of the gay subculture.

• Expanded pervert programming on television.

• Rapid expansion of the gay revolution to small-town, suburban, and rural America.

• Admittance of homosexuals and lesbians into Boy Scouts, Girl Scouts, and other private youth groups.

How do we know? The homosexual strategists tell us so in their own books and publications. Just as they told us years ago of the impending social sea-change that has now come to pass. One of the most influential manifestos of the militant homosexuals has proven to be the 1989 bestseller by Marshall Kirk and Hunter Madsen, entitled After the Ball: How America Will Conquer Its Fear and Hatred of Gays in the 90's. This theoretical and operational manual for the "overhauling of straight America" left no doubt as to the admittedly "subversive" nature of its authors' plan for "converting" America. Kirk and Madsen state: "By conversion we actually mean something far more profoundly threatening to the American way of life. We mean conversion of the average American's emotions, mind and will, through a planned psychological attack. We mean 'subverting' the mechanism of prejudice to our own ends — using the very process that made America hate us to turn their hatred into warm regard — whether they like it or not."

Sodomite Strategy

And, indeed, the buggery brain trust has been wildly successful in carrying out this "planned psychological attack." Kirk and Madsen, Harvard-trained professionals in neuropsychiatry, public persuasion, and social marketing, have shown themselves to be formidable strategists and tacticians. Their plan for "converting" America involves the systematic use of very sophisticated psychological techniques of desensitizing, jamming, and conditioning. Their book provided the step-by-step program that has been relentlessly employed — and is still being religiously pursued — to totally "overhaul" America. The authors describe the opening phase of their plan as "our recipe for desensitizing Ambivalent Skeptics; that is for helping straights view homosexuality with neutrality rather than keen hostility." "At least at the outset," say Kirk and Madsen, "we seek desensitization and nothing more. You can forget about trying up front to persuade folks that homosexuality is a good thing. But if you can get them to think that it is just another thing — meriting no more than a shrug of the shoulders — then your battle for legal and social rights is virtually won."

And how would this be accomplished? Through a massive media, public relations, and advertising "propaganda campaign." "Gays must launch a large-scale campaign — we've called it the Waging Peace campaign — to reach straights through the mainstream media," the co-authors wrote. "We're talking about propaganda." They explained to their deviate cohorts that "propaganda relies more upon emotional manipulation than upon logic, since its goal is, in fact, to bring about a change in the public's feelings."

"The main thing," they asserted, "is to talk about gayness until the issue becomes thoroughly tiresome." (Emphasis in original.) Accordingly, they said, the "free and frequent discussion of gay rights by a variety of persons in a variety of places gives the impression that homosexuality is commonplace. That impression is essential, because ... the acceptability of any new behavior ultimately hinges on the proportion of one's fellows accepting or doing it." And, the pervert pair opined, the "fastest way to convince straights that homosexuality is commonplace is to get a lot of people talking about the subject in a neutral or supportive way. Open, frank talk makes gayness seem less furtive, alien, and sinful; more aboveboard." This strategy comprehended fully the truth of Alexander Pope's observation that, "Vice is a monster of so frightful mien, As to be hated needs but to be seen; Yet seen too oft, familiar with her face, We first endure, then pity, then embrace."

Even the religious "bigots" and "intransigents" who do not "embrace" gay culture, noted Kirk and Madsen, will begin to feel more and more isolated and more reticent when it comes to expressing disapproval. And the conservative "may still shake his head and think, 'People are crazy these days,' but in time his objections will become more reflective, more philosophical, less emotional."

But — and this is all-important — the non-stop, desensitizing talk about "gayness" was meticulously designed to be a strictly controlled propaganda operation, employing not only the aforementioned sophisticated psychological techniques, but the very deliberate and massive use of the Big Lie. The Big Lie technique — repeating a gross falsehood often enough that it becomes "fact" — has been a central and essential component of the long-term campaign by the queer lobby — and its allies and patrons — to "sell" the American public the fallacies that:

• Homosexuals comprise 10 percent of the population.

• Homosexuality is an innate, genetically determined orientation.

• Science, reason, and true Christian charity affirm homosexuality as natural and virtuous.

• Homosexuals are just as "normal" as the general heterosexual society and present no moral, social, or health threat to the larger community.

• Common stereotypes concerning homosexual behavior, traits, mannerisms, dress, and sexual practices are vicious and false.

• Homosexuals are kind, loving, monogamous people, not practitioners of wild, promiscuous sex.

• Homosexuals present no more danger to children or national security than do heterosexuals.

• Homosexuals are innocent victims of an oppressive heterosexual society.

• Fairness and decency demand that "good" heterosexuals defend homosexuals from the bigotry and oppression of "straight" society.

• "Anti-gay" attitudes and moral condemnations of homosexuality constitute "hate crimes" and/or mental illness, requiring either prosecution or coercive medical treatment and "reeducation."

Lies Have Consequences

Has this campaign of "emotional manipulation" worked? Absolutely. The ten percent myth has been so frequently cited in popular literature that it has achieved the status of unchallenged dogma in both straight and deviant circles. However, there is absolutely no evidence to support such an extravagant claim. Like so many other lies concerning homosexuality, it owes its origins to the perverse pseudoscience and outright deception of Alfred Kinsey. The most generous, reliable estimates, based on surveys using scientifically recognized methodology, put the figure at closer to two percent (see "Pseudo-science Behind the Ten Percent Myth"). Of course, establishing "normalcy" by citing the percentage of the population which claims a particular belief, practice, habit, or lifestyle — whether it be 10, 20, or even 90 percent, and whether or not the figure is genuine — does not answer the more important questions concerning the moral rightness or wrongness of the belief, practice, habit, or lifestyle. Moral verities are not properly derived from polls, scientific measurements, or sociological data.

Rivaling the 10 percent myth in terms of frequency of repetition and the employment of unalloyed mendacity and bogus science is the "born gay" lie. Kirk and Madsen know this is the case but are not about to let facts get in the way of their higher purpose. "We argue," say the author-activists, "that, for all practical purposes, gays should be considered to have been born gay — even though sexual orientation, for most humans, seems to be the product of a complex interaction between innate predisposition and environmental factors during childhood and early adolescence." It's a simple matter of expediency. "To suggest in public that homosexuality might be chosen is to open the can of worms labeled 'moral choice and sin' and give the religious Intransigents a stick to beat us with," they confess. With the help of Time, Newsweek, ABC, NBC, CBS, and the rest of the prostitute press, the homosexual propagandists have been largely successful in keeping the moral choice/sin "can of worms" closed.

However, the cooperation of corrupt and radical members of the clergy also has been crucially important in keeping the "sin" stick hidden in the closet. "While public opinion is one important source of mainstream values," say the manifesto co-authors, "religious training in childhood is another. Yet two things can be done to confound the homohatred of the moderately religious." And what are those things? "First," the lavender war strategists explain, "gays can use talk to muddy the moral waters, that is, to undercut the rationalizations that 'justify' religious bigotry and to jam some of its psychic rewards. This entails publicizing support by moderate churches and raising serious theological objections to conservative biblical teachings...." Moderate churches? They mean, naturally, "progressive," "socialist," and "communist," churches — members of the World Council of Churches, and member churches of the openly homosexual Metropolitan Community Churches denomination.

"Second," say Kirk and Madsen, "gays can undermine the moral authority of homohating churches over less fervent adherents by portraying such institutions as antiquated backwaters, badly out of step with the times and with the latest findings of psychology. Against the atavistic tug of Old Time Religion one must set the mightier pull of Science and Public Opinion...."

They are confident the formula will work. "Such an 'unholy' alliance has already worked well in America against churches, on such topics as divorce and abortion," they note. And "with enough open talk about the prevalence and acceptability of homosexuality, that alliance can work for gays." As indeed it has. The above words were published, recall, in 1989. Over the past decade, we have seen pro-sodomite "Reverends" like Jesse Jackson, Mel White, Hans Venable, Larry Bethune, Jerry Sloan, William S. Coffin, Paul Moore, and many

190

others marching in Gay Pride parades and insisting that active, practicing perverts can be, at the same time, faithful Christians.

Wholesome "Everyman"

For the most part — aside from the repugnant and thuggish activities of Queer Nation and ACT-UP extremists — the Lavender Lobby has followed the Kirk and Madsen prescription to not "draw attention to the gay sex habits that provoke public revulsion." "In the early stages of the campaign," the deviant advisers admonished, "the public should not be shocked and repelled by premature exposure to homosexual behavior itself." What's more, they advised their fellow deviates to keep the "cocky mustachioed leathermen, drag queens and bull dykes," as well as pedophiles and other "exotic" gays, as far from straights and the media as possible. "Persons featured in the media campaign should be wholesome and admirable by straight standards," they insisted, and "indistinguishable from the straights we'd like to reach."

Thus, the slick public relations campaigns of the perverts generally have featured as spokespersons conservative-appearing homosexuals in Brooks Brothers suits and lesbians in Liz Claiborne-style fashions. And countless news stories, commercials, and public presentations have followed the Kirk-Madsen script, which calls for presenting "conventional young people, middle-aged women, and older folks of all races," along with "parents and friends of gays." The endless media procession of "coming out" stories has been an integral part of this plot.

"First, coming out helps desensitize straights," according to propagandists Kirk and Madsen. "As more and more gays emerge into everyday life, gays as a group will begin to seem more familiar and unexceptional to straights, hence less alarming and objectionable." They elaborated further that "coming out is a critical catalyst for the all-important 'conversion' process. Conversion is more than merely desensitizing straights or jamming their homohatred: it entails making straights to identify with them. This becomes possible when a heterosexual learns that someone he already likes and admires, such as a friend or family member, is homosexual. The discovery leads to an internal showdown between

191

the straight's personal affection on the one hand and his bigotry on the other."

And you thought that the decade-long deluge of "coming out" events was a spontaneous affair! Ha! Never has a charade been more carefully choreographed. "In order to make a Gay victim sympathetic to straights you have to portray him as Everyman," the Kirk-Madsen script explained, confident that "the press will publicize our concerns and report our news, and our community will enjoy enhanced prestige." It is the long-term, cumulative effect of many little steps that they seek: "After 'meeting' enough likable gays on television, Jane Doe may begin to feel she knows gays as a group, even if none has ever introduced himself to her personally."

In addition to the "Everyman" strategy, the Kirk-Madsen program outlined a campaign to "paint gay men and lesbians as superior — veritable pillars of society." This involves both publicizing an historical "honor roll of prominent gay or bisexual men and women," including "suspected 'inverts'" from "Socrates to Eleanor Roosevelt," and lining up celebrity endorsements. The past few years have witnessed a politically correct stampede of politicians, entertainers, authors, and intellectuals into the "pro-gay" camp, a host of celebs pouring out of the closets, and an avalanche of movies and television programs with homosexual, lesbian, and transvestite characters and themes. Singers Elton John, Boy George, K.D. Lang, Janis Ian, and Melissa Etheridge openly proclaim their "gay" identities. Homosexual movie/record mogul David Geffen (the "G" in SKG Dreamworks, with Steven Spielberg and Jeffrey Katzenberg) lavishes millions of dollars on gay/lesbian causes. Geffen, together with Fox TV founder Barry Diller, Hollywood power broker Sandy Gallin, designer Calvin Klein, and a close group of homosexual and pro-homosexual friends, comprise what has been dubbed the Velvet Mafia, which has boosted the queer content of films and television programming and helped to line up stars such as Oprah Winfrey, Madonna, Tom Hanks, Sharon Stone, Magic Johnson, Barbra Streisand, Ted Danson, and a legion of others to endorse "gay rights" or raise funds for homosexual causes. One measurement of the magnitude of their baleful influence can be seen in the willingness of macho-male stars Patrick Swayze and Wesley Snipes to take roles as prancing transvestites in the drag-queen comedy, To Wong Foo, Thanks For Everything, Julie Newmar, or of Tom Selleck and Kevin Kline to do the homosexual kissing scene in the blatant, gay agitprop "comedy," In and Out.

Admissions Against Interest

The Hollywood and media power elites have enthusiastically implemented the homosexual propaganda agenda as outlined by Kirk and Madsen. But even a cursory perusal of the homosexual press (which is about all any self-respecting "straight" can stomach) quickly reveals that the "normal," "wholesome," "victim" image is a monstrous lie. But don't take our word for it. Read what homosexual author and playwright Larry Kramer, one of America's best-known, militant gay activists, says in The Advocate, which bills itself as "The National Gay & Lesbian Newsmagazine."

In his angry essay, "Sex and Sensibility," in the May 27, 1997 issue of The Advocate, Kramer laments the fact that his fellow homosexuals, far from having learned their lesson from the plague of AIDS, are rushing promiscuously and obliviously into the abyss of destruction. "Nature always extracts a price for sexual promiscuity," says Kramer, surveying the rampant debauchery of contemporary "gay" culture. AIDS and other deadly and debilitating sexual diseases comprise a major component of that price. "Tragically, not enough of us have responded to this information maturely and responsibly," says Kramer. We cannot repeat (and have no desire to) most of Kramer's profanity-strewn jeremiad against his fellow perverts. But he makes our case more powerfully than we — or any other straight "homophobe," for that matter — ever could.

"We must create a new culture that is not confined and centered so tragically on our obsession with our [genitalia] and what we do with them," Kramer declares, while almost despairing of that lofty gay ideal. "Instead," he says, "our 'artists' just continue to perpetuate what got us into all this trouble and death in the first place." He cites, as an example, the anonymous, promiscuous sex of the then-new novel, The Farewell Symphony, by Edmund White, whom he describes as "our most distinguished gay writer." "There are so many faceless, indistinguishable pieces of flesh that litter these 500 pages that reading them becomes, for any reasonably sentient human being, at first a heartless experience and finally a boring one.... Surely life was more than this, even for — especially for — Edmund White."

Kramer vainly pleads: "Is it not incumbent, particularly in the time of a plague that has been spread by our own callous indifference to ending it, that those of us who are read and listened to perceive of ourselves as fuller human beings and capable of writing about far more than just what sex we had night after night for 30 years?" "I am so sick," he continues, "of the literature of sex, of the soft porn of all our novels and short stories that traffic only or mostly in sex. Tricks, bushes, S/M, discos, drugs, bathhouses, Fire Island, phone sex, meat racks — is that all we are capable of writing about or our audience capable of reading?"

Kramer continues to dish it out, with a vengeance:

We don't have a gay culture, I don't believe. We have our sexuality, and we have made a culture out of our sexuality, and that culture has killed us. I want to say this again: We have made sex the cornerstone of gay liberation and gay culture, and it has killed us....

We've all been partners in our destruction.... We have been the cause of our own victimization. I know these are grotesquely politically incorrect things to say. So be it. We knew we were playing with fire, and we continued to play with fire, and the fire consumed monstrously large numbers of us and singed the rest of us, all of us, whether we notice our burn marks or not. And we still play with fire.

Marshall Kirk and Hunter Madsen know that what Kramer says is true. In fact, they sound off with similar-sounding anger against rampant pervert excesses in their book. In chapter 6, "The State of Our Community: Gay Pride Goeth Before the Fall," they write: "Of all the misbehavior we decry, self-indulgence is perhaps the most characteristic of gays, and of the gay community as a whole." "Indeed," aver the deviant duo, destructive self-indulgence "was institutionalized, long ago ... as a central tenet of gay liberation." Amongst gays, they say, "any self-restraint is, itself, suspect of being a sign of self-hatred and blue-nosery — so one virtually must act out one's most fleeting impulses in order to prove that one isn't a hung-up, judgmental old poop."

Kirk and Madsen confess that they, too, formerly indulged in many excesses. But they are appalled at the wild, public debauchery and the "ongoing lavatorial passion play" in which so many gays indulge. They write:

Despite their high visibility, and attempts by authorities to squelch them, however, a coterie of gay men continues, daily and nightly, to perform the play before what is, all too often an S.R.O. [standing room only] straight audience — in the men's rooms of Ivy League Colleges, and in the public lavatories, parks, and alleyways of every major city in the United States. Theirs is the wretchedest of all gay excesses.

But the wretchedness doesn't end there. Validating what religious "homophobes" and professional psychologists alike have observed, Kirk and Madsen explicate a common problem of homosexuals:

As one gains experience, vanilla sex with one partner becomes familiar, tame, and boring, and loses its capacity to arouse. At first, the increasingly jaded gay man seeks novelty in partners, rather than practices, and becomes massively promiscuous; eventually, all bodies become boring, and only new practices will thrill. Two major avenues diverge in this yellow wood, two nerves upon which to press: that of raunch, and that of aggression. The pursuit of sexual happiness via raunch — fetishism, water sports and coprophilia, and so forth — seeks, essentially, to restore erectile thrills by restoring the "dirty," hence forbidden, aspect of sex.

But these depravities soon fail to do the trick. "Unfortunately," Kirk and Madsen say, "this, as with all attempts to sustain the furor sexualism of youth by sheer intensification of some peripheral aspect of the experience, is doomed to failure; mere amplification of 'dirtiness' results, finally, in mere wallowing in filth — which, however far the ante is upped, eventually fails to satisfy, or even to arouse." Which is why so many homosexuals then "graduate" to the even more unspeakable depravities of sadomasochism and bondage sex. "Aggressive sex," Kirk and Madsen acknowledge, "is worse than a mere dead end: in extreme cases, it's dangerous." No, in all cases it's dangerous; in "extreme" cases it's more extremely dangerous. And all too often it results in a literal dead end, as the cases of Jeffrey Dahmer, Andrew Cunanan, John Wayne Gacy, Juan Corona, Bruce Davis, Patrick Kearney, Andrei Chikatilo, Ludwig Tiene, and numerous other infamous homosexual mass murderers attest. This should not surprise, since, as Kirk and Madsen admit, the "trappings, expressions, and emotions [of "aggressive sex"] are those of pain and hate, and, say what you will, pain and hate are what it arouses."

Kramer, Madsen, Kirk, and other "responsible" homosexual moralists regularly condemn the "promiscuous" sex of their more ribald confreres. But their definitions of what constitutes "promiscuous" and "responsible" are noteworthy. "By 'promiscuous' we mean those who have sex only with anonymous partners," say Kirk and Madsen. Which would seem to leave wide latitude for sex with multiple partners — as long as you know their names. That would qualify as promiscuous in just about any heterosexual lexicon. Indeed, while even liberal heterosexuals would consider two or three sex partners per year to be treading the bounds of promiscuity, surveys of homosexuals repeatedly show that it is common for them to have dozens — even hundreds — of partners.

This mad pursuit of raw, gratuitous, non-stop sexual gratification provides no emotional fulfillment. "One of the major reasons the gay lifestyle doesn't work is that, when gays form relationships at all — and they do so far less frequently than the wishful thinking of popular mythology would have it — they form them for the wrong reasons, with the wrong people, of the wrong ages," Kirk and Madsen note. So what do these moralists offer as the "right" ages, people, reasons, and relationships? The ideal of these then-30-something authors is the pairing of "an attractive boy — of, say, sixteen or so" and "an older, presumably more mature and established man — of, say, thirty or so." And this they say even as they condemn the "youth obsession" of the larger homosexual community.

Rage vs. Love

After the prudish public has been properly "desensitized," "conditioned," and "converted" to believe that decency and justice require support for "gay rights," public hostility must be focused upon those who remain committed to traditional morality. In After the Ball, Madsen and Kirk have delineated an insidious, Orwellian propaganda program that you undoubtedly have already witnessed in operation — perhaps without even realizing it. This is what they recommend:

The best way to make homohatred look bad is to vilify those who victimize gays. The public should be shown images of ranting homohaters whose associated traits and attitudes appall and anger Middle America. The images might include:

Klansmen demanding that gays be slaughtered or castrated;

Hysterical backwoods preachers, drooling with hate to a degree that looks both comical and deranged;

Menacing punks, thugs, and convicts....

Whom do they advocate targeting for this vicious treatment? All those "denizens of bigotry's darkest realm — say, 30-35% of the citizenry" who are "vehemently opposed to homosexuality." If you fall into that category, you are considered one of "the damned."

What is the force that motivates these revolutionaries? Kirk and Madsen offer a revealing answer in After the Ball. "After all," they tell their readers, "we are asking you to change a nation under your own steam. And where, for that matter, is the steam supposed to come from? Your patriotism and sense of fair play? Your homophile zeal?... Agape? No, few are motivated over the long haul by zeal or saintliness. Yet sufficient motivation is found … all around you: the sustaining emotional steam that comes not from Love but from Rage." Yes, a hellish rage and fury drives this revolution. "Fury galvanizes," say the authors. "Now it must drive all of us to decisive action. America in the 1990s is the time and place for rage — ice-cold, controlled, directed rage."

Unfortunately, Christians have allowed Hell's rage, fury, and deception to wage war on our civilization virtually unchallenged and unimpeded. It is time to join the battle — not with rage, but with courage born of, yes, agape — love."

https://thenewamerican.com/the-queering-of-america/

Final Word

America is indeed living a lie. All of us are.

We have been lied to by the leadership of gay organizations in their 'anything goes' takeover of America.

Their organization's words are not the words of all gays, nor do they represent all gays, for many of them are distraught over the magnitude of the consequences their "anything goes" takeover has caused them, their families, their friends, and all Americans. We know this firsthand from our gay friends in the church after 50 years of service in the Episcopal Church and our experiences in truth seeking for the information and education of all persons.

We know right from wrong. When some turn away from God and the teachings of the fathers of our great nation, we must stand and stop the madness, by addressing, in a Christian manner, the issues that divide and separate us and work towards a resolution.

We must right the wrongs, because wrong has occurred. We must right them through truth, reason, and common sense, and it must be satisfactory to citizens on both sides of the issues.

We are all living these lies - homosexuals, heterosexuals, doctors, churches, schools, military, and the courts. This was all brought about by militant gay organizations using the guerilla tactics of Saul Alinsky, as predicted by Marshall and Kirk 50 years ago.

Show us the Light Lord to right this wrong with love for all persons.

BIBLIOGRAPHY

Pages 2-4   Levinson, R. S. "The 1972 Gay Rights Platform - Platform Created at the National Coalition of Gay Organizations Convention Held in Chicago in 1972." *RSLevinson.Com*, 22 May 2010, www.rslevinson.com/gaylesissues/features/collect/onetime/bl_platform1972.htm.

Pages 5-6   Reilly, Robert. *Making Gay Okay: How Rationalizing Homosexual Behavior Is Changing Everything*. First Edition, Ignatius Press, 2014.

Pages 6-8, Lyons, Richard D. "Psychiatrists, in a Shift, Declare Homosexuality No Mental Illness." *NY Times* [New York City, New York], 16 Dec. 1973, www.nytimes.com/1973/12/16/archives/psychiatrists-in-a-shift-declare-homosexuality-no-mental-illness.

Pages 9-14 Clowes, Brian, and Brian Clowes. "History of the APA on Homosexuality." *Human Life International*, 4 Aug. 2020, www.hli.org/resources/apa-on-homosexuality.

Pages 16-18 Wikipedia contributors. "Integrity USA - Biography of Dr. Louie Crew." *Wikipedia*, 3 Feb. 2021, en.wikipedia.org/wiki/Integrity_USA.

Pages 19-32 Wikipedia contributors. "Integrity USA." *Wikipedia*, 3 Feb. 2021, en.wikipedia.org/wiki/Integrity_USA.

Pages 33-37 Canon I.18 of the Episcopal Church USA Constitution and Canons.

Pages 39-43 White, Mel. "A Manifesto by John Shelby Spong." *Rev. Dr. Mel White: Clergyman, Author, Activist*, 3 Apr. 2019, melwhite.org/a-manifesto-by-john-shelby-spong.

Pages 44-36 Mohler, Albert. "The Battle Is Over?—Bishop Spong Exits the Debate." *AlbertMohler.Com*, 20 Oct. 2009, albertmohler.com/2009/10/20/the-battle-is-over-bishop-spong-exits-the-debate.

Pages 47-61 Walton, Jeffrey. "Critics Demand Young Life 'Fully Affirm Queer Relationships.'" *Juicy Ecumenism*, 14 Aug. 2020, juicyecumenism.com/2020/08/14/young-life-lgbt.

Pages 63-64 Shelly, James. "The Homosexual Propaganda Campaign in America's Media." *Truthaccordingtoscripture.Com*, www.truthaccordingtoscripture.com/index.php. Accessed 12 Mar. 2021.

Pages 65-74 Kirk, Marshall. *After the Ball: How America Will Conquer Its Fear and Hatred of Gays in the '90s by Marshall Kirk (1989-05-26)*. Penguin Books, 1989. pp. 147-157

Pages 75-80 "What You Need to Know About the 'Drag Queen' Indoctrination of Children in Your Public Libraries." *Mass Resistance*, www.massresistance.org/docs/gen3/19d/ALA-push-behind-DQSH/index.html.

Pages 81-102 "The Rainbow Book List." *American Library Association*, 10 Feb. 2021, glbtrt.ala.org/rainbowbooks/about.

Pages 106-109 Wikipedia contributors. "GLAAD." *Wikipedia*, 6 Mar. 2021, en.wikipedia.org/wiki/GLAAD.

Pages 111-115 Hurley, Lawrence. "Landmark U.S. Supreme Court Ruling Legalizes Gay Marriage Nationwide." *U.S. News*, 28 June 2015, www.reuters.com/article/us-usa-court-gaymarriage-idUSKBN0P61SW20150628.

Pages 115-117 Bourne, Lisa. "Churches That Refuse to Perform Gay 'Marriages' May Lose Insurance Coverage." *LifeSiteNews*, 10 July 2015, www.lifesitenews.com/news/churches-that-refuse-to-perform-gay-marriages-may-lose-insurance-coverage.

Pages 119-122 PSA Research. "Kenneth Cole Creates and Launches 'We All Have AIDS' Public Service Campaign on World AIDS Day." *PSA Research Center*, www.psaresearch.com/kenneth-cole-creates-and-launches-we-all-have-aids-public-service-campaign-on-world-aids-day. Accessed 11 Mar. 2021.

Pages 123-128 Foust, Michael. "Major LGBT Group Urges Biden to Strip Accreditation of Christian Schools, Colleges." *ChristianHeadlines.Com*, 19 Nov. 2020, www.christianheadlines.com/contributors/michael-foust/major-lgbt-group-urges-biden-to-strip-accreditation-of-christian-schools-colleges.html.

Pages 129-134 ---. "Human Rights Campaign." *Wikipedia*, 4 Mar. 2021, en.wikipedia.org/wiki/Human_Rights_Campaign.

Pages 150-165 Virtue, David W., and Mary Ann Mueller. "Episcopal Church's Hit List against Orthodox Clergy Tops 700 and Counting | VirtueOnline – The Voice for Global Orthodox Anglicanism." *Virtue Online*, 16 July 2013, virtueonline.org/episcopal-churchs-hit-list-against-Orthodox-Clergy-tops-700-and-counting.

Pages 166-169 Gerstmann, Evan. "Don't Panic: The Supreme Court Is Not Going To Overrule Its Same-Sex Marriage Decision." *Forbes*, 19 Oct. 2020, www.forbes.com/sites/evangerstmann/2020/10/10/dont-panic-the-supreme-court-is-not-going-to-overrule-its-same-sex-marriage-decision/?sh=ed1e112284b9.

Pages 171-180 Lawsuits Are a Symptom; the Disease Is Terminal Allan S. Haley December 14, 2008

Pages 181-182 Wright, Crystal. "The Gay Takeover of America by Crystal Wright." *Townhall*, 9 May 2013, townhall.com/columnists/crystalwright/2013/05/09/the-gay-takeover-of-america-n1591834.

Pages 183-197 Jasper, William F. "The Queering of America." *NEW AMERICAN*, vol. 31, no. 14, July 2015, pp. 36–40.

MEET THE AUTHOR
Bradley Hutt

Bradley R. Hutt is the co-founder and current Chairman of The American Anglican Fellowship Inc. founded in 1984. He was an active member of The Episcopal Church USA for 50 years in lay leadership positions in two Parishes including several terms as Church Warden. He reorganized and served as Chair of the Washington Diocesan Architectural Commission for 15 years overseeing 94 Parishes. He was a conservative church delegate and member of the press to the Episcopal Church Diocesan Conventions and General Conventions for more than 30 years. He was a Director of Engineering for a 250-member consulting firm in Northern Virginia, and designed, managed or oversaw more than 2,500 major land development engineering projects in his 45+ year career. He remains a fundraiser consultant for non-profit organizations and web designer.